COMPOST
CITY

Practical Composting Know-How
for Small-Space Living

REBECCA LOUIE

ROOST
BOOKS

Boston & London

2015

CONTENTS

4. OUTDOOR COMPOSTING: ABOVEGROUND SYSTEMS

. . . open-air bins, enclosed bins, and tumblers wow you   44

5. OUTDOOR COMPOSTING: UNDERGROUND SYSTEMS

. . . Can you dig this? Trenches, sheet composting, and digesters   69

6. THE WORMDERFUL WORLD OF INDOOR VERMICULTURE

. . . embrace the wordplay and get yourself some worms   77

7. BOKASHI FERMENTATION

. . . a pickle you want to get into   112

8. URBAN FARMYARD

. . . so many compostable animal poops in the concrete jungle!   134

9. GET ORGANIZED! COMMUNITY COMPOSTING

. . . there's no need to go solo   150

10. JOIN THE GREEN PARTY: ECO-TAINING
... more fun than hiring a clown   170

PREFACE

What would you say if I told you that reading this book and doing some of the things in it would yield the following results:

- Give you wizardlike powers of transformation over all sorts of organic matter
- Indulge your fantasies of being an overlord/master puppeteer/chief operating officer/benevolent dictator/personal trainer/positive enabler over millions of organisms
- Make you utterly fascinating to the people around you for a minimum of eight minutes* at any potluck/kids' party/BBQ/corporate function/PTA meeting/pub crawl/first date, and so on (*Actual times may vary based on an individual's speaking speed.)
- Help you save the world

Once perceived as the exclusive purview of country folks with rolling fields, composting is actually an accessible and fun activity that is transforming the landscape of even the slickest of cities worldwide.

Whether you live in a microscopic studio or a sprawling townhouse, there are many easy ways you can turn your food and garden waste into "black gold." Ready to master the art of urban composting?

Read on to find out how.

1 COMPOSTING: YES YOU CAN!

First things first.

Anyone can compost anywhere. Seriously.

Tiny studio apartments? Check.

Little kids with the attention span of gnats? Check.

Lazy, disorganized, overextended, underexercised, meat-and-Cheetos-eating, stiletto-rocking, critter-fearing, agoraphobic and/or nature-compromised city and suburban folks who have never seen a haystack or a cow pie in their lives? *Check!* (Oh, and FYI: A cow pie is not a pie made with beef but actually a poop patty. If you thought the former, no worries. You don't need to be fluent in farm talk to be a compost pro.)

You can even make a party out of it. A literal party. As in: Cocktails! Snacks! Goodie bags! Friends! (Wait until you get to chapter 10. You will soon be making edible grape "earthworms" for guests, with or without the vodka . . . trust me.)

And in case you were wondering if your book club, PTA, Zumba for Zebras charity group, or Dungeons & Dragons Wizard Council might be game to join your compost-buddy roster, the answer is also a resounding *check*. Nothing bonds a group better than playing with peels while saving the earth.

Now, you may have skeptics, naysayers, or Debbie and Danny Downers in your life who want to put a damper on your desire to compost. They keep insisting that compost

- smells bad,
- attracts pests,
- requires outdoor space,
- is a ton of work,
- makes a mess,
- takes up a lot of room,
- will make your neighbors hate you, and
- is gross.

I get it. There are some bad compost piles out there, just like there are bad eggs, bad apples, and bad brownies (just kidding, there is no such thing as a bad brownie). Compost's bad rep comes from mismanaged piles made with the best of intentions but the worst of upkeep. Plus, your experiences with the forgotten Frankendrawers in your refrigerator make you a little leery of cozying up with decomposing food.

The good news is that by reading this book, you'll learn how to easily choose and care for a compost system that fits perfectly into your (tiny) space, (busy) schedule, and (multifaceted) lifestyle. We'll also navigate the tricky, sticky situations that may arise when your composting endeavors cross paths with the uninitiated and compost wary.

Most important, you'll be armed with the information you need to ensure you *won't* become a compost train wreck.

Put your compost cap on. Whether you compost one tea bag or whole honking barrelfuls of scraps at a time, you're about to have a whole lot of fun.

COMPOST NATION

These days, *everyone's* talking about compost. Along with backyard chickeners, balcony beekeepers, rooftop farmers, and community gardeners, urban composters are part of a bumper crop of pioneers who are redefining the agri-cultures of densely packed concrete jungles. For city folks, getting "back to the land" no longer means hightailing it to the countryside on the weekend or joining a Community Supported Agriculture (CSA) group. Instead, it signals the innovation and creativity afoot as they bring the land back to themselves.

Whether they're staunch environmentalists or trendsetters touting green as the new black, city and suburban folk are putting their apple cores where their core beliefs are—in a compost pile. Across the country, thousands of households, community organizers, Master Composters, schools, and restaurants have embarked on grassroots efforts to close the circle on food waste and improve the environmental and economic condition of their city. Major municipalities (including pioneering cities San Francisco and Seattle, Boulder and Portland, Oregon) have launched government-funded programs to pick up residential food waste and enact commercial composting laws.

But why?

Back in the day, Ma Earth cooked up a savvy cycle to ensure that all creatures across all species have access to the nutrients they need to survive. It looked something like the illustration on page 4.

Over time, humankind came up with its own ideas . . . and you know what they say about too many cooks in the kitchen. Buildings, superhighways, and subway lines are just some of the ways we've interrupted the magic that occurred naturally in and on the soil. As society modernized, we lost some of this ancient logic.

How to reclaim it?

Enter composting!

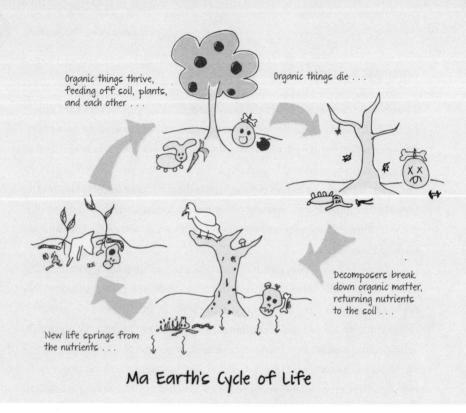

Organic things thrive, feeding off soil, plants, and each other . . .

Organic things die . . .

Decomposers break down organic matter, returning nutrients to the soil . . .

New life springs from the nutrients . . .

Ma Earth's Cycle of Life

Composting is the controlled practice of recycling the nutrients in organic materials. Compost does all bodies good—from the tiny bodies of microorganisms to the megamacroscopic body of magnificent Ma Earth herself.

Here are some of the most important ways that each small step in composting is a giant leap for everythingkind:

It's Good for the Soil

Compost is an amazing amendment that breathes life into soil. When you feed and nurture the soil, you feed and nurture everything that depends on that soil to survive—which includes you.

Soil is an elegant ecosystem made up of organic matter (called humus), rocks, minerals, water, air, and a web of micro- and macroorganisms. It's not to be confused with dirt, which is the stray stuff stuck in your sneaker treads or smeared across your jeans. Soil is rich with life, and we hold it close to our gardens and our hearts; dirt is lifeless, not useful, just stray remnants we clean away.

Healthy soil has plenty of space within it for plant roots, organisms, moisture, nutrients, and air to move through and hang out in it. Humus is to soil as hummus is to pita: utterly essential and transformative. Humus is vital in encouraging aggregates to develop. It bonds to soil particles to create aggregates that improve the structure and performance of soil. Without aggregates, soil turns sandy or clay-like, limiting plant and animal growth.

BUT! If soil gets a hearty dose of humus, say, from a pile of compost, look out!

Here are some of the amazing ways compost improves soil:

Compost provides a slow and steady release of natural nutrients. Like a fridge stocked with organic meals that never, ever empties, soil packed with compost provides everything a plant needs over the long haul. Compost is full of essentials, including nitrogen, carbon, potassium, phosphorous, calcium, and magnesium. When plants consume nutrients as needed, they grow strong, helping them defend against pests and disease.

Compost feeds and houses beneficial critters. You know how your town has a network of people that keep things in working order? There's the doctor, the police officer, the sanitation worker, that pastry chef who's open 24/7. (That last person actually doesn't exist where I live, and I desperately need him or her to. Please e-mail me if you have any leads.) Healthy soil has a similar setup. Beneficial microbes and critters love living in healthy soil. As model citizens, they help make nutrients more readily available to each other and to plants. They also defend against undesirables that cause disease or weaken plants, and they break toxins down into harmless, consumable components.

Compost improves soil structure, retaining more water and giving roots room to stretch out and grow. Have you ever watered a houseplant with cracked, dead soil and watched the water drain straight into the dish below it? Depressing, I know. And you're right in thinking something's wrong. Compost improves water retention by providing lots of nooks and crannies where water can hang out, waiting to be consumed by plants and organisms. These pockets also capture nutrients, which otherwise wash through sandy soils or get stuck in clay.

WHAT'S THE DEAL WITH FERTILIZER?

It's tempting to believe that you can nourish your soil and plants with those pretty bags and bottles of manufactured fertilizer packed full of chemical wishes and synthetic dreams. They boast optimized N-P-K (nitrogen-phosphorus-potassium) ratios, suggesting your plants will get just the right servings of these elements as well as other goodies. Just a drop here, a sprinkle there, and voilá! Superplant.

Unfortunately, these industrial fertilizers aren't quite so simple. If too much is applied, it can actually harm or "scorch" the plant's foliage or roots. Fertilizers also do not help improve soil health or soil life, which limits their long-term contributions to the ecosystem. Because they are water soluble, synthetic fertilizers drain quickly out of potted plants, or worse, out of lawns and into waterways, polluting our streams and ponds.

Want to make sure your plants and soil get what they need for the long run, while protecting the environment? You got it—compost, compost, compost.

It's Good for Society

On a save-the-planet scale, this one's a no-brainer. According to the United States Department of Agriculture (USDA), 133 billion pounds of food alone

> At events, we carry around bags of this wonderful
> compost that we create—it is just to die for—and
> another sack of typical Colorado clay soil. We get
> people to put their hands in each bag and say,
> "Imagine you were a little vegetable trying to grow.
> Which would you prefer?"
>
> **—Judy Elliot,** youth educator of Denver Urban Gardens
> Master Composter Program

went uneaten in the United States in 2010. The Environmental Protection Agency (EPA) estimates that food waste accounts for more than 20 percent of landfill weight. Toss in the countless tons of compostable landscaping, paper, and cardboard materials that also get thrown away, and we're talking serious trash. Crushed under mountains of junk, organic matter decomposes slowly and without air. Two by-products of this anaerobic (airless) process are methane—a greenhouse gas—and nitrogen-heavy ammonia. One goes up into the air, the other leaches into our groundwater, and neither is good for the environment. Plus, carting waste around the country strains the environment with its drain on fossil fuels and its subsequent exhaust emissions. Composting diverts organics from the landfill, reducing all of the above, and transforms it into something not only usable but essential.

About that methane . . . When organics are *intentionally* decomposed in controlled, anaerobic conditions, methane can be farmed and converted into an energy source. Harnessed methane currently powers towns and businesses worldwide and is a growing solution for many municipalities that tap their trash for treasure. (For more on the production of biogas, turn to page 123.)

> There are interesting community aspects to composting. It is a really intentional activity that you have to put a lot of time and thought into. It is a microcosm of the problems in the garden, and you have to work out your issues with your neighbors to set up the right kind of system.
>
> —**Chris Peterson,** executive director of GrowMemphis (2012–2014)

Composting saves money. While waving green flags touches people's hearts, waving green *money* touches people's wallets. It's amazing how saving a buck or two can motivate people to go green. Composting helps cut financial corners in several different ways. In some cases, the price of composting services can be cheaper than regular trash pickup fees or paying for drop-off at the dump. When community or backyard composters take organics away, it can be totally free. Gardeners save costs on garden soil and compost when they make it themselves. And compost-rich yards and gardens require less water, a particular advantage in dry climates with high water fees.

Composting is great PR. There's no need to be cynical about a bit of good publicity—composters deserve it. Sharing news of a composting initiative of any size shows others that you, your business, or your group is all about positive change. This feel-good quality can attract potential volunteers, funders, or future composters to your cause, spreading green goodness to all.

Composting brings communities together. Whether its giggling with your kids over the wiggly ways of an earthworm or turning a fifty-foot windrow of food scraps with twenty volunteers, shared composting experiences bring people together as they cooperate, coordinate, and communicate.

It's Good for You

Ever feel as though your eyeballs were chained to a computer screen and your rear to a chair? Can you remember the last time you got out of your head, worked with your hands, and spent some time with nature? Composting is fun and is a great reason to unplug from your devices and get into the world. Nerd out on the science, edu-tain friends and family, create a vital resource, and stop to smell the (decomposing) roses.

SOIL TESTING

So pretty, isn't it? That soil in your yard, community garden, or local park? So full of lush grass and beautiful blossoms, so black and earthy . . . Beware, looks can be deceiving.

Even the most gorgeous grounds can be contaminated with a range of metals, chemicals, and toxins that cause harm with prolonged exposure. Unsafe past or present land use, proximity to pollutants, and runoff from tainted roads and buildings can all pollute the ground.

Toxins in contaminated soils can be inhaled, ingested, and even absorbed through the skin, posing a danger not only to humans but to animals as well. The Healthy Soils, Healthy Communities project by Cornell University has shown that eggs from chickens raised on contaminated soils can contain varying degrees of lead in them. Toxins can also be taken up by plants and leach down into groundwater.

State agricultural extension offices are treasure troves of resources developed by each state's land grant universities. Extension offices provide information on local agricultural, environmental, and community issues and many offer comprehensive soil testing for a nominal fee. Because they're equipped with high-tech laboratories, they are able to accurately test for soil health (structure, organic-matter levels, nutrient fertility, pH, and so on) as well as for heavy metals, salts, and other contaminants.

To find an extension office near you, visit www.csrees.usda.gov/Extension/. Private labs and additional local universities also offer soil testing.

Got bad soil? Here are a few ways you can work with it:

- Garden in raised beds with clean soil. Give a fresh start to your edibles and ornamentals by planting (literally) above the fray.

- Remediate soil with plant power. Some plant species have the ability to uptake toxins in their foliage, removing them from the soil in a process called phytoremediation. Sunflowers soak up arsenic, alpine pennycress sucks up cadmium and zinc, ragweed pockets lead, and sugar beets absorb sodium chloride after saltwater flooding. Keep in mind that treatment zones are limited by root depth, and plants with metals shouldn't be composted and applied to your gardens as this will simply return the metals back to the soil.

- Add compost. The bustling microbes in compost can facilitate the breakdown of toxins. Plus, compost provides excellent conditions for phytoremediating plants, helping to optimize their cleaning power.

A PILE OF ONE'S OWN: OVERCOME YOUR FINAL FEARS

So, that touchy-feely, hippy-dippy Ma Earth stuff is great and all. But you still have a few needling doubts and lingering reservations about whether composting is right for you.

I Don't Have a Yard. (I Don't Even Have a Private Bathroom...)

Rural and suburban homes with sprawling yards and outdoor space as far as the eye can see have the luxury of square footage, making composting a no-brainer. Compost piles can be tucked over yonder on that acre, under such and such tree, or behind the two-car garage.

But cramped city dwellers? Not so much. You live in a peanut shell atop a six-floor walkup with four other people, a cat, and a garter snake. Where on earth are you going to score space to play with decomposing food?

Don't sweat it. If your living quarters are as crowded as a rush hour subway car, you still have great composting options. Every nook, cranny, closet, drawer, underbed, overfridge, and spare square foot can provide an opportunity to compost. Clear out the clutter and make room for composting. If you haven't made a loaf in the bread machine yet, chances are you never will. Donate or sell your unwanted clothes, shoes, books, and gadgets so others can reuse as you reduce. Then fill your world with what's most important to you (hint, hint: composting).

Red wiggler worms (chapter 6), bokashi fermentation (chapter 7), and innovative machines (chapter 4) provide quick, easy, and efficient means of composting scraps indoors. If you're determined to compost outdoors, sometimes all you need is a few inquiries to get permission to set up a compost site on someone else's land. Learn how to scout locations and woo the compost wary into your web in chapter 9.

I Have Nowhere to Put the Finished Compost. (I Don't Have a Garden . . .)

No one wants to be all composted up with nowhere to go. Even if you don't have access to a yard or garden where you can use your compost, there's hungry soil everywhere you look.

Feed potted plants, share with gardener friends, supply street trees caged in the sidewalks. Or donate finished compost to gardens, schools, and other community centers with green spaces that could use nourishment. Good soil is a scarcity in concrete jungles, and your finished compost will always find a good home.

There may be a few laws or regulations you may want to consider before donning your compost fairy bonnet and sprinkling the town with

Needy soil is closer
than you think!

black gold (check out page 158). But for the most part, giving away compost is like swapping seedlings, garden harvests, or cuttings with local gardeners—a generous act of sharing and going green as a community.

I'm Not the Outdoorsy Type

Or bug type. Or nature type. In other words, you prefer the concrete jungle to the wild one, desperately devoted to modern conveniences and stylish accessories. Composting seems . . . a tad . . . inelegant, no?

What if I told you there are systems where your compost pile would largely, if not entirely, be hidden from view? And that in some cases, you don't even have to touch the compost until it's time to harvest it—if you choose to harvest it at all. In fact you can even convince buddies to do compost work for you with a simple offer of pizza and a six-pack. (Mmm. Pizza.) Ta-da! The thrill of composting without doing very much at all!

I Don't Have Time to Deal with It

There are as many ways to compost as there are people who do it, and composting fits into a range of different lifestyles. Not every compost system is a big old hill of scraps that requires a pitchfork and a lot of sweat and time to turn (though that can be a lot of fun—just saying). Some passive compost systems allow you the flexibility to tend to your compost as infrequently as every few weeks or months, or next to never.

Once you get rocking and rolling, I wouldn't be surprised if you discovered composting is a lot more fun and rewarding than you originally expected. It's like potato chips (but healthy): you think you'll eat just one, and suddenly the entire bag is gone. Composting is addictive.

Turn to the next chapter and start discovering why.

2 WHAT IS COMPOSTING?

Like your favorite cocktail or chocolate chip cookie, compost has a special recipe that, when done correctly, yields a sweet finished product and knee-knocking glee.

Here's the basic concept.

MA EARTH'S ORIGINAL RECIPE FOR BLACK GOLD (AKA COMPOST)

1 part nitrogen-rich greens

30 parts carbon-rich browns

Several parts micro- and macroorganisms

    (species vary based on recipe)

Water (as needed)

Air (optional for decomposition, see below)

A bit vague, yes, and therein lies all the fun. There are many methods of composting and plenty of room for compost chefs to improvise. No two piles are ever the same, and there is no single, absolute way to do it right. The simple guidelines in this book will help you find the most fun and effective way for you.

Here's a breakdown of the essential ingredients.

TO AIR OR NOT TO AIR?

For most life-forms, it's a no-brainer—yes to air, please! However, a range of microorganisms do just fine without air, thank you. This group includes key decomposers, especially bacteria, that can break down organic matter in unexpected, airless environments.

When people speak of backyard and small-scale composting, they're usually talking about aerobic systems that encourage air-loving microbes to come on in and join the decomposition party. Most aerobic systems incorporate manpower, machine power, critter power, or simple exposure to the elements to circulate air throughout compostable materials and get things breaking down. The result, when done right, is sweet-smelling, earthy compost.

If you get friendly with fellow aerobic composters and start talking shop, you may hear them lament the day their pile "went anaerobic." Essentially, anaerobic decomposition means air cut got off from some part(s) of their pile, and a population of microbes that love *la vida* airless moved in. Organic matter still broke down, albeit more slowly, and the process created ammonia, methane, and other by-products along the way that most people usually find unpleasant.

This book focuses mostly on building and maintaining aerobic composting systems but highlights a few anaerobic concepts to deal with organic material in chapter 7. Whether you choose Team Air or Team Airless comes down to personal choice and what fits best in your lifestyle. If you manage your system well, you'll get great compost for your plants and divert organics from the waste stream either way.

WATER, WATER EVERYWHERE!

Water is a boon for many living things. It contributes to cell structure, provides a pathway for travel, and is a key compound in many chemical reactions.

When compost piles get too dry, microbial activity slows down. When piles get too wet, water clogs air space, creating the anaerobic conditions described above.

Monitoring and managing the amount of water in your compost pile is one of the keys to successful composting. Water-rich greens such as food scraps provide your pile with its predominant food source. Dry browns like autumn leaves and shredded paper absorb moisture from greens and any additional rain or humidity your compost encounters.

Ideally, compost has a moisture content of roughly 45 to 65 percent water. Precise moisture levels can be calculated through weighing and drying compost, juggling numbers, and doing math. Blah! My head aches just thinking about it, so allow me to recommend these simpler methods of determining moisture levels instead.

- Squeeze a handful of compost. If water oozes out, it's too wet. If it falls to the ground in a dusty powder, it's too dry. If it sticks together but doesn't drip, hooray! It's in good shape.
- Think of Armando the Wrung-Out Sponge. Every cause needs a champion, and Armando is compost's moisture crusader. (Well, it's compost's moisture crusader for this book.) Perfect compost feels like a wrung-out sponge to the touch, and what better way to remember this than with the thought of Armando whispering rakishly in your ear, "My dahrlinggg, eet is perrrrfect" or "A bit too dry, my brother. Add some water, yes?" Is Armando a bit hokey? Maybe, if you're the type who doesn't love handsome sponges uttering sweet compost nothings in your ear. Is Armando unforgettable? Absolutely, and that's the most important thing. Whenever you're in doubt about your compost's moisture content, just think of Armando's damp, sexy skin. Let him guide you!

Meet **ARMANDO** the wrung out sponge...

Armando is both handsome and helpful,
a mnemonic device for the quality of good compost.

COMPOST RAINBOW: GREEN + BROWN = BLACK GOLD

Greens and browns are the goodies you rescue from everyday life to transform into fabulous compost. They're the scraps at the end of a meal, the shipping box that arrived at your door, even the fur you just brushed off Fluffy.

Greens, as they're called in the compost world, provide essential nitrogen with which plants produce proteins, enzymes, and chlorophyll for photosynthesis. It also plays a role in reproduction and growth. Common greens used in composting include food waste, grass clippings, and manure. Greens are a great source of water for your pile; think of a watermelon rind or a mango peel—that's juicy stuff.

Strawberries

Cabbage

Banana Peels

It's easy being 'greens': Fruits and veggies have plenty of a-peel in a compost pile.

Browns, on the other hand, are dry, carbon-rich materials that include paper, cardboard, dead leaves, and wood chips. Carbon, often called the building block of life, provides energy for microorganisms to do their thing, like runners carb loading with huge plates of pasta before a big race. Dry browns also perform practical roles in a compost pile: they absorb excess liquids that drain out of greens and provide a cozy blanket, or biofilter, that absorbs odor and blocks pests.

In Ma Earth's original recipe, *anything* made of organic material could be added to the decomposition mix. But in her original world, a dead animal could lie peacefully in an open field until a web of big and small decomposers chomped it down into little brittle slivers of bone. Somehow, I don't see today's condo boards or community gardens signing on to let you throw food scraps wherever inspiration hits.

While everything organic does decompose, that doesn't mean everything organic *should* decompose in your compost pile—especially when your pile lives in a shared or public space.

Here's a trusty chart featuring common compostables that will help get you on your way. I recommend starting with easier items to ensure a smoother start to composting, then advancing to more tricky substances as you become more experienced.

COMMON BROWNS AND GREENS

Get to know how different browns and greens behave in your system and curate compost ingredients to optimize moisture levels, troubleshoot problems, and affect the rate of decomposition.

Knowing the quirks of individual items is particularly helpful if your compost system has limited space or is in proximity of wary or sensitive neighbors.

EASY ITEMS THAT BREAK DOWN QUICKLY

Greens:

Grass clippings

Salad greens

Banana + peels

Coffee grounds and filters

Tea bags, with staples removed

Apple cores

Strawberry tops

Peeled fruit (except citrus) and vegetable skins (carrot, apple, potato, etc.)

Browns:

Dry autumn leaves

Non-waxy paper, including newspaper

Non-waxy cardboard boxes

Cardboard egg cartons and beverage trays

Paper towel, toilet paper, and wrapping paper rolls

Sawdust from untreated wood

Coffee chaff

Non-oily bread, pasta, and grain

Dried flowers

Very Wet Greens:

Watermelon + rinds

Cantaloupe + rinds

Honeydew + rinds

Celery

Tomatoes

Cucumbers

Plums

ITEMS THAT ARE SLOW TO DECOMPOSE

Greens:

Big pits (peach, plum, avocado, etc.)

Avocado skin

Carrots (whole or chunked)

Corncobs

Browns:

Sticks, twigs, and logs

Pine needles and cones

Wooden chopsticks and stirrers

GREENS WITH NATURAL ODOR

Garlic

Onion

Cabbage

TRICKY GREENS THAT REQUIRE SPECIAL HANDLING

Manure

Citrus rinds (a no-no in vermicomposting)

Meat

Bones

Dairy

Cooked food

Oily food

Weeds

Note: See chapter 7 about composting meat, bones, dairy, and
    prepared foods.

NEVER EVERS

Diseased plants and flowers

Poisonous plants such as poison ivy

Materials exposed to toxic chemicals

Cat manure and litter

WHERE TO SCORE BROWNS AND GREENS

Maybe you don't cook or eat produce that yields lots of peels, cores, or
rinds. You may have a paperless household, meaning there are no news-
papers to shred, no cardboard boxes to cut up. And leaves? You don't even
have a tree on your block, much less a pile of leaves to hoard.

Never fear. The beauty of a city lies in its bounty. If you're low on
compostable items, consider the following:

- Crowdsource: Ask your immediate circle of friends if they would be willing
  to save their scraps for you to compost. Provide a list of the items you'd like
  and a bag or container to store them until you can pick them up.

- Work your workplace: Make a few trips to the company's coffee machine for grounds and filters, or let coworkers know you find their leftover peels quite appealing. Keep a lidded airtight container on hand for storing scraps and clean it out daily. No one wants a whiff of last week's banana peels when you open it to add more.

- Hit up a local restaurant, café, juice bar, market, or other food-related company and see if they'd be game for collecting and sharing their food waste. (More on collaborating with businesses and groups in chapter 9.) Many coffee shops, including big chains like Starbucks, gladly give away their spent coffee grounds to gardeners. Call ahead to see if they can save up a bunch for you, or be spontaneous and just drop in. Keep in mind that grounds might be fresh and very hot, so bring a container that can withstand heat and hold liquid drippings.

CAFFEINATED COMPOST

Addicted to caffeine? So are a group of savvy composters, gardeners, and businesses in Austin, Texas. The city's grassroots Compost Coalition and the Texas A&M AgriLife Extension office created Ground to Ground, an entirely volunteer network that diverted more than eight tons of coffee grounds a month within its first year alone.

The concept is simple. Hit up cafés and other locations that generate a lot of java. Provide them with buckets to collect their grounds. Organize a network of gardeners, greenies, and landscaping lovers to pick up the grounds for their soil. Have them return the empty buckets when they're done and swap out for a fresh load.

Coffee grounds make a great addition to a compost pile—and to your soil. They're packed with vital nutrients, including nitrogen, phosphorous, and potassium. With a carbon-to-nitrogen ratio of about 20:1, they make a pretty decent stand-alone compost source as they break down.

Here's Heather-Nicole Hoffman, founding member of the Compost Coalition, on how they percolated this project:

Tea Bags and Coffee Grounds

*Create a compost brew-haha
with your morning coffee and tea.*

"Ground to Ground started with a man named Shane Genziuk in Melbourne, Australia. We contacted him and said, 'Hey, this is great. Do you think we can use your plan?' He was completely onboard and sent us what materials he had, and we developed some of our own.

"It drives me crazy to see anything go to waste, especially if you get a benefit like compost, in which everything grows better. I got involved in Meetup groups and met someone who culled blemished produce from Whole Foods. I started lining people up to get the compostable stuff and thought: let's start trying to find other places that aren't already composting.

"Small businesses are a lot easier to approach because they can make the decisions themselves. I found you just have to start talking to somebody, and then they say, 'Oh, that's a great idea!' Anytime we start with a new business, we try to make sure we have a couple of volunteers who are willing to go by once a week, twice a week, to check on them. It gives the employees a chance to ask questions.

"We talked to our local health department and got a rundown on what people need to be doing within their food establishment to stay within health department regulations.

"The Compost Coalition is all volunteers; there is no monetization along the way. All the buckets we use have been donated by the county jail. They were going in the trash before, and now they have inmates cleaning the buckets. Once the inmates knew what they were doing it for, we heard good feedback. The community gardeners can stop by and take grounds from any of the participating locations, first-come, first-served. Volunteer participation can ebb and flow, so you have to have some hard-core people willing to do it on a daily basis for a week at a time. If people aren't stepping up, you pick up the slack.

"Coffee is a great way to get people to start thinking about composting, and it is really easy. And coffee shops don't like taking the grounds out because they are heavy and often in plastic bags that leak. It has been a really good program for everyone involved."

For more information, visit compostcoalition.com and groundtoground.org.

MEET THE ORGANISMS IN YOUR COMPOST

While browns and greens are essential to composting, they only provide the venue and the buffet. A vast web of critters, creatures, and itty-bitty beings do all of the work of transforming browns and greens into black gold. Composters fondly refer to them as the F.B.I.: fungi, bacteria, and invertebrates.

Check out their dossiers.

Fungi

Why did the mushroom get invited to the compost dance party?

Because he's a fungi (geddit, fun-guy?) . . . and he can sure break it down!

Fungi are microorganisms that include molds, mushrooms, and yeasts. Common in cooler temperatures, they do a great job of decomposing cellulose and lignin, the woodier components of plant matter that can be too dry, acidic, or low in nitrogen for bacteria to work on. Fungi perform this vital task by squirting enzymes into their food and noshing on the nutrients released in this process. This occurs predominantly in mesophilic temperatures, which range from 40 to 110 degrees Fahrenheit. Fungi are most commonly found in compost made from leafy, woody materials. If you'd like your compost to be more fungally dominated, make sure to work lots of landscaping waste into your pile.

Bacteria

Bacteria are single-celled microorganisms that exist virtually everywhere. In fact, they are inside your body *right now,* about a hundred trillion of them, or ten times the number of cells you have. (Are you freaking out? Don't.)

In a compost pile, bacteria do most of the decomposition work. Mesophilic bacteria chow down on sugars and starches and are most productive in a temperature range of 70 to 90 degrees Fahrenheit. Most backyard compost piles are mesophilic, taking their temperature cues from the ambient air. As mesophilic bacteria eat, they produce heat, and the temperature of the compost system begins to rise. If they achieve temps of about 104 degrees, it gets a little too warm for them and their population dies off.

But when a door closes, a window opens, and through it charge heat-loving thermophilic bacteria. These are the dudes behind what you've heard of as hot compost piles. These powerhouses survive temperatures up to 160 degrees and plow through proteins, fats, and complex carbohydrates such as the cellulose in plant matter. Per EPA guidelines, once these sauna-like conditions reach over 131 degrees for three days, the heat successfully kills off weed seeds and pathogens—two big bonuses that solve problems posed by mesophilic piles.

Eventually, thermophilic bacteria tear through their food supplies, and their activity and population slow until they disappear. The compost's temperature decreases and another mesophilic phase returns. The cooler bacteria, along with their fungi pals, clean up anything the hot guys left behind.

One particular group of mesophilic bacteria that shows up around this time gets a special shout-out. Actinobacteria, also known by its earlier classification actinomycetes, are a special group of bacteria that appear as a cobwebby, fibrous fuzz. Like fungi, actinomycetes have enzymes that can break down tough debris like stems and bark. If you see some in your compost pile, take a sniff. These bacteria create the yummy smell associated with healthy earth.

Invertebrates

What invertebrates lack in backbone, they make up for in guts. Countless invertebrates, a mix of creepies and crawlies that might otherwise give you the chills, plow through your compost pile consuming organic matter and microorganisms. After this stuff travels through their digestive systems, what's pooped out is incredibly nutrient-rich matter that breathes life into soil.

Mites, grubs, insects, spiders, and slugs are just some of the invertebrates that dig through, chew, digest, and mix the material in your compost pile. But the superstars? Earthworms. It's possible that you've only seen them floundering on sidewalks after a good rain, but in areas rich with foliage like the forest floor, earthworms are essential in transforming organic matter into food for soil.

This process can actually be replicated in containers in your own home using a method called vermicomposting. Chapter 6 is dedicated to cohabitating with these wiggly wonders and harnessing their quiet, efficient power to transform fruit and vegetable scraps into luscious compost.

PUTTING IT ALL TOGETHER: COOKING UP COMPOST

Now, back to Ma Earth's original recipe. You'll recall it goes like this:

1 part nitrogen-rich greens

30 parts carbon-rich browns

Several parts micro- and macroorganisms (species vary based on recipe)

Water (as needed)

Air (optional; not needed in anaerobic piles)

In general, too many greens in an aerobic compost pile cause a backlog that microbes and macroorganisms can't consume quickly enough. This results in the unappealing anaerobic conditions described earlier.

On the flip side, too many browns result in a dramatic slowdown of activity. Without the water and nitrogen offered by greens, there's little incentive for fast-working bacteria to move in and do their job. While an excess of browns doesn't cause any unpleasantness for your pile, it may seem like an eternity before you get any usable compost. As it stands, passively maintained piles (which you'll learn about in later chapters) can take months to produce compost. If you fail to add enough greens, it could take years.

In general, finished compost has a carbon-to-nitrogen ratio of 30:1. What does that mean? Every brown and green out there has its own unique carbon and nitrogen content count. Coffee grounds are roughly 20:1; sawdust is about 500:1.

See where this is going? Numerical brain freeze!

I'd rather *eat* a pineapple than figure out its carbon-to-nitrogen ratio and how it affects my compost pile's C:N balance. To make sure my compost piles are balanced, I follow these simple guidelines:

- Use more browns than greens
- For every handful of greens, add two handfuls of browns.

Remember, it's always easier to add water to a compost pile than to take it away. Err on the side of caution and be generous with your browns. In time you'll be able to tell by the look and feel of your compost whether it needs more of one than the other. (Don't you worry: there will be more on this in later chapters, as it pertains to different systems.)

And remember, if you're wondering if you've hit the right balance, think of Armando the Wrung-Out Sponge. He will never steer you wrong.

3 THE VERY BASIC CONCEPTS BEHIND MAKING COMPOST

So we've been dreaming about our destination: the land of lovely, fluffy, fabulous compost. Now it's time to map out the journey you'll take to get there.

Composting requires a few basic things:

1. A place to compost
2. A strategy on how to feed, tend, and harvest the compost
3. An investment of time, energy, and resources befitting the strategy you choose

The good news is there are as many ways to compost as there are people who want to do it. This chapter explores the core concepts of making compost, and highlights key considerations to keep in mind when choosing the system that works best in your space and lifestyle.

HOW TO CHOOSE YOUR COMPOSTING SYSTEM

Compost systems are a bit like children: while they all need to be fed, watered, and occasionally cleaned up, some require a lot more maintenance and attention than others.

Knowing yourself and your limitations is key when choosing a compost system. Be realistic about how much time and energy you plan to invest in your new hobby and what kinds of resources are available to you to help make this project work. If you're not sure how much you want to commit to this endeavor, I'd suggest you assume the most minimal engagement. Underestimating means there's little chance you'll overcommit or overextend yourself.

Here's a list of key issues to consider before you start:

- **Location:** Where will you set up your system, and who might it affect? Do you need permission to be there from a landlord, a co-op or condo board, or an owner? And are there any special health, sanitation, or local ordinances that you should consider? More information pertaining to these questions, as well as tips on wrangling permissions and access, is in chapter 9.

- **Size and space:** How much room do you have to set up your compost system? In addition to the physical dimensions the actual system takes up, do you also have space to manage and harvest your pile? If you plan to use supplemental tools such as shovels, tarps, and sifters, do you have someplace to store them? Also, some systems have special needs, such as soil or room to turn or tumble the contents. Last, is there room for you to expand your operation as you become more skilled (and obsessed) with mining black gold?

- **Scale:** What types of browns and greens do you plan on composting, and how much of them do you have regular access to? (If you plan to compost meats, dairy, and cooked leftovers, turn to chapter 7; these items do not belong in the aerobic systems described in the upcoming chapters.) If you cook several vegetarian meals for a family of four every day, you've probably got an impressive mountain of peels and scraps piling up. If your idea of "cooking" is microwaving a frozen lasagna, then you may need to scrounge scraps from others to get your pile in gear. (See page 21 for how to crowdsource food scraps.) Adjust your system to the amount you will be processing, or if your volume of compostables exceeds the space you have for composting, prepare to compost just a portion of your scraps. There's no shame in running a small pile, as every little bit does Ma Earth good. It's more important to successfully manage and enjoy your pile than to create a monolith you can't control.

- **Time:** Play with your compost as little or as much as you like—there's a system for every schedule. If you want to devote lots of time and energy to composting, there are plenty of chores to do to optimize compost production. However, if you'd prefer to go to happy hour than haul scraps, there are plenty of "lazy" or busy-lifestyle-friendly ways to compost as well.

- **Cost:** Compost systems can be supercheap when handmade using freecycled, recycled, and upcycled materials. To appease your inner handyperson, basic assembly plans are included throughout this book. If you don't have an inner handyperson, there are countless makes, models, and styles available for purchase. Retail bins can climb up into the hundreds of dollars, depending on the bells and whistles that you crave. Read reviews and forum posts about the different models to learn the pros and cons that everyday folks have encountered with them. Be as savvy a shopper with your composting gear as you are with your fridges, cameras, and TVs.

- **Pest proofing:** Rats, squirrels, raccoons, roaches, snakes, and stray dogs and cats all love a good open compost pile as a source of food, shelter, and warmth. Mice, roaches, flies, and spiders may take a liking to a worm bin you set up indoors. Does the system you choose provide a way to defend against the particular critters in your environment? If not, do you have the ability to add the upgrades you need? The systems described in this book include tips on keeping wild things at bay.

BASIC MAINTENANCE FOR ANY COMPOST SYSTEM

It's game time, and the playbook is simple. The core concepts of making compost are feeding the system, turning and mixing the compost, harvesting finished compost, and curing and maturing your harvest.

Feeding the Pile

Over time and feedings, you'll get acquainted with how the dry and wet materials mix in the environment you've provided. In some systems, you will strive to achieve an Armando the Wrung-Out Sponge–type balance. In others, the formula won't be as essential.

There are detailed instructions on feeding specific systems in later chapters, but here are three general tips to keep in mind when feeding a pile:

1. The smaller the items are that you add to your bin, the faster they will break down. If you're so inclined, chop up greens and shred browns to speed along the process. Doing so increases surface area for organisms to work on.
2. If you're getting more odor or wetness than you (or your neighbors) would prefer, add more browns.
3. If action in your pile has slowed to a painstaking crawl because it's dry and dusty, add more water and/or greens.

LEACHATE

When compost piles get wet enough to leak, the resulting liquid is called leachate. This potent potion is made up of water from your greens, the liquid by-products of F.B.I. activity, nutrients and minerals, and if applicable, rain. Depending on the type of system you choose, leachate may collect in a special compartment or drain back into the soil.

Some people use the term *leachate* synonymously with the term *compost tea*, which in itself has become a catchall phrase for any number of liquid concoctions that use some combination of compost and water. (I offer a recipe for Aerated Worm-Compost Tea on page 87.) Take this phraseology with a grain of salt, because leachate isn't always the innocuous and refreshing drink a "tea" might suggest. Some gardeners swear by it as a tonic for their plants. Others have bemoaned pouring the phytotoxins or acids leachate may carry onto their prized petunias. It's a toss-up. If you do try feeding your leachate to plants, I would recommend diluting it at least twenty-five parts water to one part leachate before adding it to any soil, just to be cautious.

Turning the Pile

While turning a compost pile isn't mandatory, it sure can be helpful, even if done once in a blue moon. When browns, greens, and the F.B.I. get shaken and stirred, several valuable things happen:

1. *A peek into the abyss.* The outside of your pile may be pretty, but it doesn't always give you a true indication of the beast that lies within. Find out if your pile has gone anaerobic and smelly from too many greens or if it's gone absolutely nowhere because it's bone dry.
2. *Moving unfinished material.* The items on the periphery of your pile are farthest from the core's action and are likely breaking down slower. Turning the pile puts them in contact with the organisms hard at work.
3. *Circulating air.* Aerobic compost likes to breathe, and a healthy turn is literally a breath of fresh air for the microbes within. The CO_2 produced as a by-product of microbial processes can escape as invigorating O_2 sweeps back in.
4. *Introducing moisture.* If it's a little dry and slow at the center of your pile, a turn gives you the opportunity to take a hose or watering can to its innards.

A good turn helps ensure that your pile stays in working order. And thanks to some cool products, it doesn't have to break your back. Sure, you can still labor the old-fashioned way by plunging a pitchfork or Compost Crank into your compost. However, user-friendly contraptions like compost tumblers (page 64) and indoor machines (page 77) make light of hard work. In vermicomposting (page 77), hundreds to thousands of worms wiggle through your waste, churning and turning it as they go.

If you're taking a passive approach to composting, this step is completely optional. While it definitely helps you get to know your pile and speeds efforts along, your balanced browns and greens will eventually break down on their own.

Harvesting and Sifting the Compost

It's the moment you've been waiting weeks or even months for. The apple cores and shredded junk mail have finally disappeared, leaving behind beautiful, crumbly, moist, magical compost. It's time to scoop it up and feed it to plants and soil in need.

Knowing when to harvest your compost is pretty straightforward. Harvest when you see finished compost and (1) your system is full, *or* (2) you feel like harvesting, even if your system isn't full, because—yippee!— you have compost.

Depending on the type of system you choose, either your finished compost is deposited in a designated collection area or you have to work to get to it. The latter usually requires the use of a sifter to separate the fine particles of finished, stable compost from larger browns and greens still decomposing. Backyard composters usually use sifters made of a metal mesh, like hardware cloth, with grid holes anywhere from $1/8$ to $1/2$ inch or more. The smaller the hole, the finer the compost. I've seen some awesome do-it-yourself (DIY) versions, including people-powered bike sifters and repurposed dresser drawers. (Turn to page 36 for more DIY ideas.)

To sift compost, place your sifter above a container such as a bucket or a wheelbarrow. Shovel compost onto it. Shake your sifter or run a gloved hand over the material to urge finished material through the mesh. Bigger, uncomposted pieces remain on top. Put them aside for later, when you'll

Helpful Compost Tools

Chopper

Slice through thick stems, rinds, chunks, frozen compost, and ice. The smaller your compostables are, the faster they will break down.

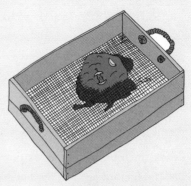

Compost Sifter

Separate finished compost from items that still need to break down

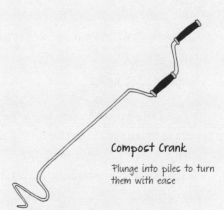

Compost Crank

Plunge into piles to turn them with ease

toss them back on the pile to finish their transformation. Repeat until you've gone through all the material in your bin or you've maxed out and gotten bored or tired.

Sifting is a great activity to do with friends or a group. To lighten the load, promise your famous strawberry shortcake (made ahead for the occasion) or a bottle of bubbly to entice the crew to help. Consider giving gift bags of compost or potting soil mixed with compost as a thank-you. (For more eco-taining ideas, turn to chapter 10.)

Easy Upcycled Compost Sifters

Ready for repurposing at its finest? Nab one of the below items and—BAM!—instant sifter. These everyday items do a decent job of sifting—with various degrees of refinement—as is:

- Milk crates
- Plastic mesh flats or trays from garden supply shops
- Discarded grates from outdoor grills
- Mesh trash cans with spaces at a minimum of ¼ inch

If the holes in your found sifter are too big, line them with a piece of hardware cloth that has the mesh size you'd prefer.

"Finishing" Compost

It looks like finished compost. It feels like finished compost. But is your compost really ready to feed to the plants and soil in your garden? Compost is a living ecosystem of micro- and macroorganisms constantly in flux. Despite its appearance, it may still be too active, acidic, or volatile to use right away.

What's an eager gardener to do?

Here are two ways to determine whether your harvested compost is ready:

1. *Bag it:* Put a small sample of your "finished" compost in a plastic bag and seal it up tight. (A sandwich bag with airtight closures is perfect for this.) Forget about it for a few days. When you revisit it, open the bag and take a whiff. If your nostrils meet a balmy breeze of earthy air, it's ready to use. If it's got the stinky, ammonia smell of anaerobic microbes at work, then it needs more time to complete the job. Return the sample to the harvested compost and let it sit for a week or two. If you'd like to help things along, turn or mix it periodically. (Remember, turning isn't mandatory, it's a nice extra.) Repeat these steps until your compost passes the test.

2. *Get cressed out:* Garden cress, an edible herb, is a robust germinator that bursts forth with baby greens in as few as four days. To test your compost's readiness, gather containers to plant a minimum of forty garden cress seeds. (I recommend easy-to-upcycle materials such as take-out containers or yogurt cups with drainage holes poked in the bottom.) Plant half of the seeds in compost and the other half in regular potting soil, taking care to label the planting medium of each container. Plant a minimum of twenty seeds in each medium, with the same number in each container. Water, and wait. If less than 80 percent of your seeds sprout in the compost flat and closer to 100 percent blooms in the potting mix, then your compost isn't ready yet. Let it sit for another week or two to allow microbes to finish the job. Repeat these steps until your germination rates improve.

Once your compost is finished—that is, it passes the tests above—have a field day using it. Or allow it to cure in a pile or in an aerated container, where it sits while activity slows. During a curing phase, the pH neutralizes, particle size decreases even further, and excess moisture continues to evaporate off the pile. Depending on your compost needs, you can deploy curing compost at different phases. Newly finished compost with lots of activity is great for dense clay soil in need of organics. A stable, fine compost, well cured, is the perfect top dressing for a delicate plant with fine roots.

THE DIY COMPOSTING SETUP

While many amazing, efficient, and good-looking composters are available for purchase, you can cut costs or walk the reduce-reuse-recycle walk by building a compost setup yourself.

Sprinkled throughout these chapters are instructions for the easiest, breeziest, and most minimalist ways to build the systems they describe. These DIY options are great for folks with limited funds, limited time, and/or limited experience (and interest) in construction. They also provide a great starting point for you to dream up your perfect bin.

The key to a successful DIY project is access to the right materials and tools.

Sourcing Materials

No doubt you have heard the saying, One man's trash is another's treasure? Well, when you live in a packed city or suburb, there's a whole lot of potential treasure out there. Browns and greens aren't the only things that are easy to acquire from neighbors, local businesses, and complete strangers. Building supplies perfect for compost systems are in abundance.

Freecycle, Recycle, and Shop Secondhand

Many compost supplies are easily scored for free or almost free. To find them, hop online to check listings on sites like craigslist.org, freecycle.org, recyclinggroupfinder.com, and finder.trashnothing.com. Pound the pavement to inquire at local businesses or put up flyers in busy locations like supermarkets and coffee shops. It's amazing how thrilled and cooperative people can be when a composter offers to take away their "junk."

When sourcing materials from strangers, safety first. Connect in public places, bring a friend if possible. Also, find out as much as you can about the materials you're picking up. Previous use or storage conditions can contaminate items with chemicals or other pollutants that you may not want to expose yourself or your compost to. Here's a list of some of the best pickin's out there:

- **Wood shipping pallets:** Pallets provide great free lumber to build bins, raised beds, sifter frames, and more. They aren't made of the highest-quality wood, but they're readily available and easily replaced if they wear out over time. Confirm that the pallets you snag are heat treated—not chemically treated. Heat-treated pallets will be stamped with the International Plant Protection Convention (IPPC) logo and HT for "heat treated." Chemically fumigated pallets will be stamped MB for the pesticide (and neurotoxin and respiratory threat) methyl bromide—which you do not want to handle. Pressure-treated wood is also a no-no because it may be treated with toxins, including arsenic, that can leach into the soil and air. Paint can also be a concern if you'd prefer to not have paint residue in your compost. If you have any doubts about a pallet, don't take it.
- **Food-grade buckets and barrels with lids:** Buckets and barrels make excellent tumblers, worm bins, digesters, container-garden planters, and more. They're also great for storing and hauling compost, browns, greens, and other supplies for gardening. Many food service businesses and cafeterias receive bulk ingredients in food-grade containers and toss empties out in the trash. Rescue them and give them new life.
- **Cinder blocks:** Stack 'em, shape 'em, and paint 'em for fun. Cinder blocks are readily available for easy, no-muss no-fuss building of simple structures. They also weight down bin lids, helping to protect compost from pests and the elements.
- **Milk crates:** Recycled milk crates aren't just good as makeshift bike baskets. Take advantage of their holey structure for compost sifting, or use these hardy cubes for storage. Line them with landscape fabric to make worm houses or growing beds.

Helpful DIY Tools

5-Gallon Buckets

Transform a bucket into a compost system or use it to haul and store items.

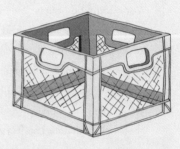

Milk Crates

Crates are great for many compost and gardening needs.

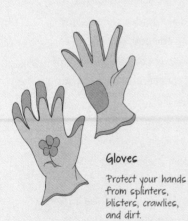

Gloves

Protect your hands from splinters, blisters, crawlies, and dirt.

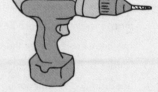

Drill

What can't you accomplish with a drill in hand? Look for DIY instructions throughout this book wherever you see this drill.

Most of the DIY projects in this book can be constructed with the materials described above, a drill, and a few other easy-to-get odds and ends. Work gloves, which are sturdier than garden gloves, are also great to have on hand (and on your hands!) to keep your manicure safe and to protect you from splinters and pointy things.

THE MAKING OF MASTER COMPOSTERS

Across the nation, thousands of individuals have undergone a special training called Master Composter certification, learning the ins and outs of backyard and community composting. Master Composters wield their pitchforks and trowels, leading millions of microorganisms and invertebrates (plus a good number of people) in the battle to transform organic waste to soil.

The Master Composter program was designed by Carl Woestwin, Jeff Gage, and Craig Benton during the 1980s through sustainable food advocates Seattle Tilth. Over the years, the curriculum has been tweaked and iterated upon to serve the needs and interests of many cities and towns.

Here are pioneers Carl Woestwin and Jeff Gage on starting their revolutionary program:

Carl: "The genesis of the program was out of Seattle Tilth. I worked on developing the Tilth garden at the Good Shepherd Center in Seattle. We started in 1977 working with the community. It took several years before our parks department agreed to have an urban gardening demonstration site there. All along the idea was to have a composting demonstration as part of that.

"The wave of interest in urban agriculture we were riding in the late '70s, early '80s was rising with the interest in alternative technologies. There were lots of graphics of people with rooftop greenhouses, windmills on rooftops. Aquaculture was a really hot new item then. In the last maybe eight to ten years, it has come back with a vengeance, focused more around the idea of regional food, with urban agriculture as a subset of that, and the desire to close the loop on site when possible.

"In '85 the city of Seattle published a request for proposals [RFP] looking for a community composting education program. We responded to that RFP and got it.

We started working on a manual for the program, developing a composting demonstration site and the training manual for the Master Composters, and set up a compost hotline. We looked in part at the Master Gardener program. That was really the model for the Master Composter program. We were also looking at Bill and Helga Olkowski and the whole thing they were doing with [their urban sustainability book] *The Integral Urban House.*

"Our first class was in '86, and it has been going continuously since then."

Jeff: "The early days were very interesting. We decided we needed to make the message of composting simpler. We decided not to include esoteric [compostable] products like hair because we just wanted people to make a pile, keep it moist, and allow those with more enthusiasm for composting to get into the hairy details."

Carl: "When we started the program, we talked a lot about hot composting and three-bin systems. But with time, we grew to realize that there are very few people who are going to take the time to do that kind of composting. For the larger number of people, a passive system where you can add material over time makes much more sense. That's why we use the terminology of greens and browns. We started out talking about carbon and nitrogen ratios, and it's just too much information."

Jeff: "We worked out approvals of food-waste composting methods with the local health departments and came up with the direct burial, trench, and worm-bin methods. This changed into the Green Cone method in later years. We only encouraged food waste in the yard waste bins if they were being turned once a week and managed intensively and placed in an enclosed compost bin system. It was important to come up with methods that were acceptable to the health officials and were no-brainers for the users."

Carl: "One of the challenges of an urban area is the nuisance complaints. Odor can be a challenge, and rodents are a huge challenge. That's why, when we started the program, we recommended not combining food and yard waste. Even though it will compost better combined, if we get the health department breathing down our neck, we're in a ton of trouble. We need to be really conservative with what we tell people. There are two separate systems—yard-waste bins and worm bins, Green Cones, or another type of digester system for food.

"For an urban person working a job, maybe with kids, with all of the distractions of an urban environment, keeping up with your organic wastes and doing it properly takes time. If I were shaping the education [today], I would just say be really practical about what's possible and what a large number of people are able and willing to do."

For more information, please visit http://seattletilth.org.

4 OUTDOOR COMPOSTING: ABOVEGROUND SYSTEMS

Open-Air Bins, Enclosed Bins, and Tumblers

If you had a home where the buffalo roam and the deer and the antelope play, you could probably just toss all your food and yard waste out to the gentle herbivores and the elements and call it a day. However, it's more likely that where you live, the closest thing you have to an antelope is the cantaloupe you purchased presliced from the corner deli. And as for roaming wildlife . . . city pigeons, squirrels, rats, and roaches don't really have that same pastoral-chic appeal.

Believe it or not, outdoor composting is entirely manageable, fun, and rewarding in crowded city and suburban spaces. Even if you don't actually have a garden or access to soil, you can still transform food and yard scraps into gorgeous black gold. You just have to apply a little innovation and metropolitan moxie to make sure it goes smoothly.

Outdoor compost systems are surprisingly flexible. With the exception of a big thermophilic pile, which requires a certain amount of square footage and volume to achieve optimum performance (more on this later), outdoor systems can be adapted for many different spaces:

- Backyards, front yards, and side yards
- Patios and cement walks
- Balconies
- Rooftops
- Driveways
- Alleys
- All of the above that belong to friends and families
- Local parks and municipal spaces
- Schools
- Community gardens
- Abandoned lots
- Businesses with green space

  (Information on how to negotiate shared, public, and private spaces belonging to others is in chapter 9.)

Not too shabby!

This chapter covers ways you can compost aboveground in these spaces with open-air compost bins, enclosed compost bins, and compost tumblers. (The next chapter digs a little deeper by exploring subterranean systems in which compostables are deposited underground.)

BATCH AND CONTINUOUS COMPOSTING

Off the bat, you have a choice: to batch compost or to continuous compost.

In batch composting, you fill your system to the hilt all at once, care for it as instructed, then harvest it all at once. This method appeals to folks who want a shorter route to finished compost and/or who have access to a high volume of compostables at once. By depositing browns and greens when there's a full batch, a busy person can limit how often he or she visits the compost bin.

Continuous composting is an ongoing method where browns and

greens are added to a system in small portions, whenever the whim or need strikes. The result is a compost pile that, over time, has a combination of finishing or finished compost and browns and greens in various stages of decomposition. Most backyard piles are maintained in the continuous method. Its low-maintenance approach is great for people with minimal scrap volume who aren't in a rush for finished compost.

All of the systems described in this chapter can be batch or continuously composted. Experiment with your volume and time and see which method works best for you.

Open-Air Compost Bins

Open-air structures hold compostables together in a highly ventilated structure that is largely exposed to the elements. Open bins are particularly useful for people with space who crave easy access to turn, tweak, harvest, and generally admire their pile. The most popular open-air bins are wire holding units and single or multistage bins. Before getting into the nuts and bolts of caring for each of these types of system, take a peek at some best practices that apply to both systems.

General Location

Open bins are easiest to manage when placed directly on soil. Direct contact with the ecosystem below encourages microbes, bugs, and earthworms to crawl up into goodies you've supplied and get the decomposition process started. Soil bottoms also do wonders for drainage, sucking up any excess liquids from water-rich greens and rain. Because soil is penetrable, it is easy to anchor an open bin in it. This is particularly helpful for lightweight wire holding units.

If you're setting up an open-air compost bin on concrete, lay down a tarp or other protective barrier to prevent the bin contents from staining the surface below. A few inches of soil or finished compost between the tarp and the first layer of browns and greens helps absorb excess liquids and jump-start microbial activity.

General Feeding

Remember that 2:1 brown-to-green ratio we discussed in the previous chapter? To start, do that when you feed. Then cover your contribution with several inches of browns, as many as eight inches if possible. This carbon biofilter serves as a barrier to pests and helps to block odors—both boons to the neighborhood. During future feedings, simply dig into the center of your pile, bury your greens, and cover them back up with your brown layer. Toss the appropriate ratio of browns to new greens onto the top of the pile to maintain balance.

Closed-toed shoes protect your feet from compost, muck, and tools.

Adding Worms

Whether you're on soil or concrete, consider adding a handful or two of red wiggler earthworms to your open bin. They're not mandatory, but they do wonders to break down and aerate material. Plus, they multiply insanely fast. Don't worry if your pile gets hot in the center; the worms will move to the periphery, where temps are friendlier and the food is bountiful. If you're set up on soil, they'll simply migrate underground and return when conditions are more comfortable.

General Pest Proofing

The "I'm so exposed" nature of open bins is a tempting invitation for pests of all shapes and sizes. If you have a lot of unsavory critters in your area, modifying your bin will go a long way toward pest proofing and please neighbors and Negative Nellies. (For more community considerations, check out chapter 9.) One of the easiest ways to prevent creatures from squatting in your pile is to line any openings, cracks, holes, and ventilation slats of your bin with quarter-inch hardware cloth secured with a system-appropriate fastener like a sturdy staple gun or zip ties. Is your bin top-less? Consider adding a lid or an additional layer of hardware cloth across the top. A pallet lined with hardware cloth, plywood, a tarp, or a bit of spare roofing material can do the job. Be creative with recycled and up-cycled materials.

Now that we've got the basics down, let's get into the particulars.

Wire-Mesh Holding Unit

THE DIRT ON WIRE-MESH HOLDING UNITS

- Ideal for yard waste
- Not good for food scraps
- A passive, low-maintenance system
- Easy to set up, break down, and transport
- Can be adapted to fit in a range of spaces

If mowing your lawn or raking your leaves results in minimountains of clippings, consider corralling all of that great compost fodder in a wire-mesh holding unit. This simple structure is typically made with wire mesh such as hardware cloth or chicken wire that is secured in a cylindrical shape with stakes.

Feeding

Adding greens and browns to your pile is simple. Fill up your wire-mesh holding unit with yard waste and let nature do the rest of the work breaking it down. Because food scraps don't go in this system (it's too flimsy to fend off determined and crafty city pests), you don't have to pay as close attention to balancing your greens and browns. Yard waste doesn't contain nearly as much water as, say, a summer's worth of watermelon rinds. There are rarely moisture, leachate, or anaerobic issues to balance. In fact, many people fill holding units with piles of autumn leaves (a common brown) alone. The eventual result is crumbly, wonderful compost that resembles the goodness Ma Earth makes on the forest floor.

Maintenance

If you're inspired, periodically mix your pile to circulate air, moisture, and organisms throughout the pile. Reach over the top of your wire-mesh wall and stir things up with a pitchfork or plunge a Compost Crank into the leafy depths and give it a whirl. If it's more comfortable for you to turn your compost from the side, unhook one length of your mesh and swing it open like a door, allowing side access.

DIY: WIRE-MESH HOLDING UNIT

Making a wire-mesh holding unit is easier than pie because, as you know if you've ever tried, making a pie can be a pain. These systems are easily customized to fit the

Pruners

Cutting tools like pruners help reduce the size of twigs and bulky yard waste.

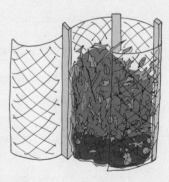

Wire-Mesh Holding Unit

Compost leaves and yard waste in this simple setup. Remember, never add food waste to this system.

size and space available. You get to call the shots on how tall it stands and how wide its circumference is.

YOU WILL NEED:

- Work gloves to protect your hands
- Pliers
- Hammer
- Length of galvanized chicken wire sized to the circumference of your desired holding unit, plus an additional 6 inches
- Galvanized wire lengths or zip ties to use as fasteners
- 3–4 wooden poles that are the height you'd like your unit to be, plus an additional 6 inches if you are building on top of soil (see note)
- 3–4 cinder blocks if building on a nonsoil surface
- Rope if building on a nonsoil surface
  Note: Upcycled lumber pieces are a great free option, or you can purchase T-posts or U-posts—which have convenient hooks for attaching to wire—from a hardware or gardening store.

BUILDING THE HOLDING UNIT:

1. Fold back 3 inches on the cut ends of the chicken wire so the edges are smooth and unlikely to poke you or catch on your clothes.
2. Stand the wire in a circle so the folded edges touch.
3. Use fasteners to connect the edges to each other, along the entire height of the tube.
4. Space the poles around the inside of the unit so they touch the wire.
5. If you are building on soil, hammer your poles into the ground about 6 inches. Then tie the poles to the wire with fasteners.
6. If you are building on concrete, tie the poles to the wire with zip ties. Then position the cinder blocks around the outside of the unit. Thread the rope through the wire and cinder block holes to anchor the unit in place.
7. Proceed with care and maintenance as described on page 49.

Single and Multistage Open Compost Bins

THE DIRT ON SINGLE AND MULTISTAGE OPEN COMPOST BINS

- Best option for thermophilic (hot) composting
- Great for active people who want a system they can work with aggressively
- Can also be used for passive composting
- Needs pest proofing if you're adding food waste
- Can be adapted to fit in a range of spaces

Put a few walls around your compost pile and—voilà!—a compost bin is formed. Open compost bins are usually square structures made of wood boards, cinder blocks, or metal mesh squares with either three walls and an open side or three walls and a "door" side.

Open bins work wonders in pairs or triplets. When one bin is stuffed to the gills, leave it to finish while adding fresh material to a new bin. By the time the new bin fills up, the original pile will have broken down significantly (especially if it is being aggressively maintained with frequent turning and moisture maintenance). If the original bin needs more time to finish composting and you've got more room, go wild and start a third bin. This classic three-bin system is one of the most popular outdoor composting methods around.

Common in community gardens and in the backyards of prolific scrap makers, open bins are your best bet for creating a hot compost pile. When built to specifications of three feet by three feet by three feet, dimensions determined by composting pioneers as the optimum space ratios, these bins most effectively achieve the toasty conditions required to kill pathogens and weed seeds. They also get stuff breaking down fast. (More on this on page 54.)

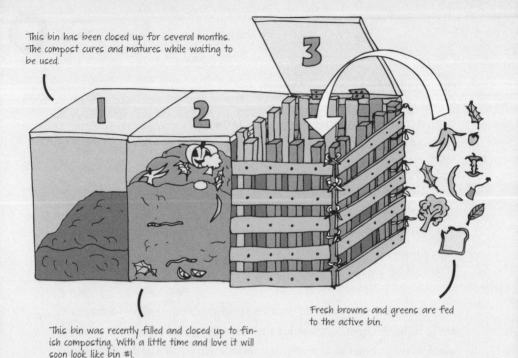

This bin has been closed up for several months. The compost cures and matures while waiting to be used.

Fresh browns and greens are fed to the active bin.

This bin was recently filled and closed up to finish composting. With a little time and love it will soon look like bin #1.

Three-Bin Composting System

Feeding an Open-Air Bin (Continuous Composting)

Add your greens to the bin. If you're adding a lot of greens at one time, mix in a bit of brown to help prevent anaerobic conditions.

Try to maintain a layer of browns eight inches thick at the top of your pile to serve as a thick pest and odor barrier. For future feedings, make a pit in your browns, bury your greens, and cover them back up with the brown layer that had previously been there. Add more browns to the top in the 2:1 brown-to-green ratio to keep balance.

Maintenance (Continuous Composting)

If you choose to turn your pile and peek inside, don't cause a stink in your neighborhood. Sometimes turning a pile can mean unleashing the odors of its potentially smelly core. Pockets of tightly packed and/or overly wet greens may have gone anaerobic. Or the mountain of onions from your "French Onion Soup Fete" may cause a naturally stinky storm. For the sake of good citizenship, think twice about turning your pile on the afternoon your next-door neighbors are hosting a BBQ on their terrace.

But what's a do-gooding greenie to do when the call to turn compost overwhelms or your friend bails for lunch and a long, lonely afternoon looms? Charlie Bayrer, who processes tens of tons of New York City residential food waste in giant compost windrows as a cofounder of Earth Matter (see page 137 for more on the group), has a quick tip: use a compost thermometer. A compost thermometer is a long, thin tool people plunge into the center of the pile to monitor internal activity and determine whether mesophilic or thermophilic bacteria are at work. Bayrer suggests, "If you're working with a compost thermometer, smell the tip when you pull it out of your pile. That will tell you whether you really want to open the pile and expose the rest of the world to that smell. You might want to wait for a shift in the wind or wait another week to see if it smells any better."

(see page 137 for more on the group)

Repeat (Compost) Offenders

Onions

Garlic

Broccoli

Onions, garlic, and broccoli are common odoriferous greens that stink naturally as they decompose.

One caveat on turning your pile: If you're maintaining a bin during winter months or in a cold climate, it's possible that exposing the warm core of your pile may actually end up releasing more heat than it can regenerate once it's put back together. If you're trying to maintain a certain temperature and level of activity, you may wish to wait for a balmier day.

FEELING HOT, HOT, HOT!
CREATING A THERMOPHILIC OPEN-AIR PILE

Some like it hot in their compost piles—like, 131 to 160 degrees hot. At this sweltering temperature, weed seeds and pathogens are destroyed, leaving the remaining compost hassle-free for use. Compost piles heat up when ravenous thermophilic bacteria move in and tear through browns and greens, transforming them into compost.

Bedding Fork

Bedding forks are an alternative to pitchforks and are helpful for scooping and turning finer particles.

Looking to create a thermophilic pile? Robert D. Raabe, a professor at the University of California, Berkeley, has created the "Rapid Composting Method," which is commonly known as the Berkeley method. Using batch compost, this approach produces finished, weed- and pathogen-free compost in about three weeks. Not bad compared with the months, if not years, a passively managed pile can take.

Here's how he does it:

Day 1: Fill up your 3 x 3 x 3–foot bin with layers of brown and green materials in a 1:1 ratio. The pile should heat up within twenty-four to forty-eight hours.

Day 4: Check the temperature at the center of your pile using a compost thermometer. If it's 131 degrees plus, you're doing it! If not, you may need to add more green material or water to jump-start it. Turn the entire pile, making sure to move cooler, less decomposed material from the outer edges into the hot core. As you expose inner layers, check the moisture content. If it's too dry, add more water. If it's too wet, add more browns.

Every subsequent two days: repeat Day 4 steps.

Day 18: By this time, your pile should have reduced dramatically. If it's not completely finished, it's nearly there. Yay, you did it!

Note: Frequent turning makes it hard to maintain the eight inches of browns as a biofilter you would otherwise keep on an outdoor pile. If you're composting in a pest-ridden area and/or have sensitive neighbors, pest proof your bin on all sides, including the top.

NATUREMILL INDOOR HOT COMPOSTING

If you don't have the space or scrap volume to hot compost outside, consider turning the heat on in your very own kitchen. The NatureMill is a small electric machine with two compartments. The top heats browns and greens (including cooked food, meat, dairy, and pet waste) up to 140 degrees and periodically mixes them. The bottom collects and cures finished loads. Yes, a machine that does all the work of composting for you . . . if only it also did the dishes.

NatureMills work both indoors and outdoors, provided they have access to electricity, making them a flexible contraption for a vast range of people. They fit in cabinets and under tables and come in discreet shades of black and chrome. NatureMills cost about fifty cents a month in electricity to run, and the price tag for a unit, which comes in several models, runs a few hundred dollars. This may be cost prohibitive for folks hoping to compost on the cheap, but it is a great option for those willing to pay for a hassle-free experience. For more information, visit www.nature mill.net.

Alternative Uses for Compost Heat

Turning the heat up to kill weed seeds and pathogens is impressive in itself. But who knew hot compost could get this cool? Compost heat can be put to good use in many interesting and surprising ways:

1. Build a hot compost pile in a greenhouse to take the edge off winter's chill or to help extend the growing season during spring and fall.
2. In spring, seedling flats that are set atop a hot pile feel warm and toasty and show their appreciation by sprouting sooner.
3. Got serious construction chops? Run pipes of water through a hot-compost heap and reap the benefits. Architects, engineers, and regular old handy-folks have created hot-compost water heaters that can be used to warm houses, wash dishes, and more.

Harvesting Compost from a Bin

The contents of your bin are black and crumbly, and there is nary a peach pit to be found. It's time to harvest.

If the oldest pile in your multibin system is finished, or if you've batch composted, harvesting is a piece of cake. In these conditions, your browns and greens have run a full course (taking weeks to months, depending on how passive you were). All you need to do is shovel finished goodness directly into a bucket or wheelbarrow. Bonus points if you sift it first.

If you've been continuously composting, a bit more work awaits. Your finished compost is likely mixed in with browns and greens in various states of decomposition.

- If you haven't been turning your pile, pull off the top layers of newer, less decomposed materials and set them aside. Sift the dark, compact, finished

RUB-A-DUB-DUB, A COMPOST HOT TUB

Even though hot compost is not for everybody, the experience of building a hot-compost pile is really exciting for most people. It's eye-opening that it can reach those kinds of temperatures. [In the early days at Seattle Tilth], we built a giant compost pile using wood chips and manure and whatever we could find. We had PVC pipe running through it and a pump hooked up running water through that system. We ran the water into our greenhouse and lined one of the raised beds with black plastic and made it into a hot tub. It was fun! People would say, "Wow, you mean those microbes in the compost pile heated a hot tub?" And I'd say, "Yeah, that's how hot it gets!"

—**Carl Woestwin,** cocreator of the United States' first Master Composter Program with Seattle Tilth

layers below. Once you've harvested it all, return the unfinished content to the bin.

- If you have been turning your pile, your new and finished material will be pretty well mixed throughout. Simply stick in your pitchfork or shovel and start sifting.

Check the readiness of your compost using the cress or plastic-bag test. Curing is optional.

DIY: OPEN-AIR PALLET COMPOST BIN

This simple outdoor bin is cheap and easy to assemble and disassemble, and can house a hot-composting pile.

YOU WILL NEED:

- 4 heat-treated pallets of the same size (see page 39 for tips on sourcing safe pallets)
- Additional pallet, plywood, tin roofing, or the like to use as a roof over the top of the bin (optional)
- Rope or galvanized wire
- Hardware cloth for pest proofing, enough to line the surface of all four pallets plus the bottom of the pile and, if using one, the lid (optional)
- Staple gun to affix hardware cloth to pallets, if pest proofing

MAKING THE BIN:

1. Select or make a flat surface outdoors for your bin.
2. If you are building on soil, lay down hardware cloth over the bottom surface so pests can't burrow into your pile from underneath (optional).
3. Attach hardware cloth to each pallet on the side you'd like to face inward, including the lid if you are using one (optional).
4. Position 3 pallets together in a sideways U shape atop the hardware cloth you laid on the ground. If you used hardware cloth on your pallet walls, make sure the hardware cloth faces the inside of the bin.
5. Using your wire or rope, tie the pallets together at the corners where they meet, securing them the entire height of the pallets.
6. The fourth pallet will be the front door to your bin. Position it with the other pallets to create a box. Tie it in a way that makes it easy to either swing open or completely remove the door for turning or harvest.
7. Top the bin with a lid (optional).

8. Manage your compost following the instructions on page 52.

9. If you would like to expand to a 2- or 3-bin system, get 3 additional pallets for each bin you'd like to add, plus an additional pallet for any lids you'd like to include. Follow the steps above, using one wall from your first bin as a shared wall with the next.

DIY: OPEN-AIR CINDER BLOCK BINS AND GARDEN BEDS

Who says grown-ups can't play with blocks? Inexpensive, easy to work with, and insanely durable, cinder blocks can be arranged into many practical compost structures. Simply decide on the dimensions you need for your open bin or raised-bed composter (more on raised-bed composters in the next chapter) and stack your blocks. Plus, cinder blocks are easy to paint to match your outdoor decor.

Most cinder block bins have three sides, with the fourth wide open for turning and harvesting. After all, opening and closing a cinder block door would be tough on the biceps. Having an open side may be seen as an open invitation to lunch by some pests, so consider creating a pest-proof door and lid from a pallet and hardware cloth or composting only yard waste in this kind of bin.

Enclosed Outdoor Systems

Sometimes you just need to shut the door, close the windows, and hide away from the world. If you'd like your compost tucked away discreetly, consider an enclosed outdoor system.

Usually made out of plastic or metal, enclosed bins are minimally ventilated structures that neatly and completely encase your compostables. There are two main types of enclosed systems discussed in this chapter: enclosed bins and tumblers. They're not bad looking, even handsome at times, and they shield onlookers from the maze of twigs, leaves, orange peels, and corn husks within. The discretion factor comes in handy when you live in a crowded neighborhood, keeping your new hobby from becoming an eyesore or nosesore to neighbors and passersby. Because these systems are self-contained and easily assembled, renters and other temporary residents will appreciate their portability. Typically, there's a door to put compostables in and another door to harvest from. In some cases, these openings are one and the same.

Location

Enclosed systems provide a lot of flexibility in terms of where you can put them, especially if you develop a custom-sized system to fit that cranny behind the garbage cans, to the left of the bush.

Tumblers and systems with bottoms are particularly suited for balconies, rooftops, patios, sidewalks, and other cement or tiled surfaces. Bottomless bins work optimally when placed on soil.

Sunlight will always help warm your compost bin and the microbes in it, but it isn't required.

Feeding

Generally, enclosed systems are fed in a 2:1 ratio of brown to green. If you have a soil bottom, you may even be able to add more greens, as any excess liquids will simply leach into the ground.

Enclosed systems with bottoms, such as tumblers, tend to retain a lot more moisture. This can make contents heavy, mushy, and sometimes stinky. As you get to know your system, adjust the ratio of brown to green as moisture levels require. A generous supply of browns go a long way in combating glop.

If it seems like the inner processes have come to an utter standstill, the pile may be too dry. Whip out the watering can and give it a good shower.

Maintenance

Batch and continuous composting are both suitable for enclosed compost systems. Tumblers spin and mix your browns and greens with the bare minimum of help from you. Enclosed bins lean toward total passivity, but you can turn the pile if their top opening is big enough or if you have a hankering to take the bin apart a bit.

Pest Proofing

Enclosed composters are built like citadels, and they're great for pest prevention. If you're concerned about pests getting through any ventilation openings, cover them up with hardware cloth.

Enclosed Compost Bins

THE DIRT ON ENCLOSED BINS

- Discreet systems that shield composting contents from public view and the elements
- Low maintenance
- Good for balconies, rooftops, and other tight spaces (fully enclosed versions)
- Requires attention to brown and green balance (fully enclosed versions)

Often set atop soil but customizable for other surfaces, enclosed bins are basically aerated columns or cubes that you feed from the top through a lid or door. As material is added to it, creating layers of browns and greens within, finished compost begins collecting toward the bottom of the bin. Depending on the model or style of the bin you choose, finished compost is harvested from a door or hatch at the bottom, or the entire bin is emptied at once.

Enclosed Compost Bins

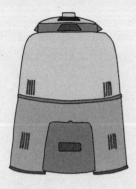

In this common style of enclosed bin, scraps are added through the top hatch.

Harvesting compost is easy when your enclosed bin has a hatch at the bottom.

Location

Bottomless bins work best when placed directly on top of soil but can be set up on any surface. If starting on concrete, be sure to place a few inches of soil or finished compost at the bottom to absorb any liquids that may drain from your greens. If you're worried about staining the ground surface, set the unit up on a waterproof tarp.

A fully enclosed bin with bottom provides more ease and flexibility. Set it up on soil, on your balcony, or on the sweet rooftop that is the envy of all of your friends.

Feeding

Start by feeding your bin two parts of browns to one part of greens as often as portions become available. You can even err on the conservative side, using more browns than you would in an open system. Keep in mind these structures do a good job of containing moisture . . . sometimes too good. Between the non-porous materials they're made from and the small ventilation holes inherent to the system, there's little room for moisture to escape into the atmosphere. If it ends up too wet in your system, made evident by odor and/or pooling liquids, then add more browns. If the contents are dry and dusty, you may need more greens or a sprinkle of water.

If you've achieved Armando the Wrung-Out Sponge balance, pat yourself on the back and go get an ice-cream cone.

Remember, there's no universal formula for achieving the perfect balance of greens and browns: temperature, humidity, the size and number of ventilation holes, the types of scraps you put in your bins and the density of the microbial population will all affect how quickly items break down.

Maintenance

Enclosed bins make great passive systems that generate compost in several months. Time, of course, varies depending on what and how often you feed the pile, whether you turn the contents, and environmental factors such as temperature. While you're off at the club or doing kung fu, the materials break down on their own. If you'd like to speed up the process or you just like to be involved, reach in through the top opening to mix your bin's contents with a Compost Crank, pitchfork, or hand rake.

Harvesting

Many enclosed bins have a door or hatch at ground level, providing access to older, more-composted material. When it's time to harvest a bottom-opening bin, simply slide open the door and shovel out as much compost as you have (or are willing to deal with). If the compost has a lot of chunky items in it, give it a good sift and return the big particles to the bin. Gravity pulls less-finished upper layers down, where decomposition will continue until your next harvest.

If you choose a system with a single opening, such as a DIY enclosed bin made from a bucket, you'll have to shovel or dump the contents out and sift them. Batch composting comes in handy for single-door systems.

DIY: ENCLOSED COMPOST BIN

Enclosed compost bins are among the easiest to construct, and custom bins can be tailored to fit many locations. If you intend to manage this system aggressively by turning its contents often, choose a container you can easily reach into for mixing (or consider making a tumbler with the instructions in the next section).

YOU WILL NEED:

- Trash can, bucket, or barrel with a tight-fitting lid
- Drill with a ¼-inch drill bit
- Safety goggles if you are drilling into galvanized metal

BUILDING THE BIN:

1. Drill ventilation/drainage holes throughout the sides, bottom, and lid of your container. Space them 5–10 inches apart.
2. Cover the bin with the lid.
3. Follow the feeding and maintenance instructions above.

Compost Tumblers

THE DIRT ON COMPOST TUMBLERS

- Discreet systems that shield composting contents from public view and the elements
- Low maintenance with potential for high-yield results
- Good for people whose physical ability to turn compost is limited
- Good for balconies, rooftops, and nonsoil surfaces like concrete, tile, and so forth
- Requires attention to moisture

"To everything—turn, turn, turn . . . ," or let a compost tumbler do it for you.

Tumblers are compact, efficient systems that provide solutions to many of composting's vexing inconveniences. They come in barrels, balls, wheels, and drums; I've even seen a bright pink one in the shape of a chubby pig. Because tumblers are designed to roll or turn easily, they spare people the labor of manually mixing the compost bin by hand. This replaces a major step in active composting with an insanely passive approach. Tumblers also fit in many places without fuss, including balconies, rooftops, and the slim alleys between apartment buildings.

Because tumblers are entirely enclosed, they provide a great barrier between your food scraps and the curious creatures that want to eat them.

Feeding

Tumblers can get quite wet inside, inviting all sorts of unpleasantness. Avoid this problem from the outset by taking care during your feedings.

Start by feeding the bin in a ratio of two parts browns to one part greens. Close it up and give it a tumble. During your next feeding, take a peek inside. Is there a lot of condensation on the walls? Visible pools of liquid or drips trickling out the tumbler door? Does it smell not so amazing? Are the contents stuck together and gloppy? These are all hints that your system needs more browns. Add them, give it a tumble, and check again in a few days. Paying close attention to conditions during your first few feedings will go a long way in helping you balance your bin in the long term.

A tumbler's factory-clean environment is void of soil microbes. Jump-start the microbe action by tossing a handful of soil or compost into your tumbler. Do not add worms to a tumbler, because they don't have a buffer zone to take refuge in should temperature or moisture extremes arise inside.

Maintenance

Good news! The inherent tumbling aspect of a tumbler makes turning your compost a cinch, eliminating a lot of hard work and offering a great payoff. And the good news continues for lazy folks who will be glad to hear that they never really have to tumble their tumbler if they don't want to.

Some styles of tumbler sit on a reservoir that collects leachate that drains out of your scraps. If you opt for this style, be sure to check and empty this reservoir periodically.

Harvesting

Your tumbler's getting pretty heavy; you can feel it each time you spin the crank or roll the wheel. It's time to harvest!

If you composted in a batch, just pop open the hatch, pour the contents onto a tarp or into a bucket, sift, and enjoy.

If you've been composting continually, the chances are your tumbler will contain finished compost and fresh scraps. Sift the contents of your tumbler to separate out the finished compost. Then return the unprocessed scraps back to the tumbler so they can continue to break down.

 DIY: COMPOST TUMBLER

Ready to roll? Most commercial tumblers are affixed to a hinge or wheel that allows you to turn them in place. This DIY version requires enough space so that you can you roll it on the ground or down the sidewalk. All tumblers get heavier as you fill them up, so work with a size you are comfortable placing on its side, rolling around the ground, and righting again.

YOU WILL NEED:

- Cylindrical trash can, bucket, or barrel with a tight-fitting lid
- Drill with a ¼-inch drill bit
- 2 bungee cords (if using a trash can)

BUILDING AND USING THE TUMBLER:

1. Drill ventilation/drainage holes throughout the sides and bottom of your container. They can be spaced 5–10 inches apart.
2. Add browns and greens as described on page 19.
3. Cover the bin with its lid. If you're using a trash can, secure the lid by crisscrossing the bungees across the top and hooking them onto the trash-can handles.
4. To tumble the contents, tip the tumbler on its side and roll it around the yard or along the sidewalk.
5. Once you're done, set it back upright and store it in its usual place.

As you can see, there are plenty of fun and fabulous options for outdoor, aboveground compost systems that fit many spaces and lifestyles. The added benefit, which can't be overstated, is

Compost Tumblers

If you strap the lid down on this enclosed system, it becomes a DIY tumbler!

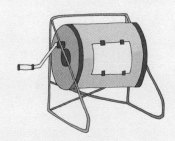

Crank it up! This style of commercial tumbler turns with arm power.

Leachate conveniently pools in the reservoir below on this style of commercial tumbler.

that you get to spend time away from your computer, TV, or vacuum cleaner and out in the fresh air.

However, not all spaces (or communities) lend themselves to visible monuments to decomposition's greatness. An aboveground bin may take away from a landscaper's elaborate design or hog the one spot where the grill fits.

All is not lost. The next chapter goes deeper into outdoor composting options. Much deeper. Like, a foot or two underground deeper. Read on.

5 OUTDOOR COMPOSTING: UNDERGROUND SYSTEMS

Can you dig this?

Submerging your scraps directly in soil may be the simplest way to compost. It's discreet and doesn't require balancing greens and browns. If you have the space, it can also accommodate large volumes of scraps. Once set up, underground methods are low maintenance. No turning, watering, or pest proofing? No problem!

Underground systems are great for people who

- have outdoor space with access to ground soil or deep raised beds
- have little time for or interest in a high-maintenance system
- don't want a big, visible pile to take up aboveground space or disrupt the landscape.

Here are the three main methods for underground composting:

1. Trench composting
2. Sheet composting (aka lasagna gardening)
3. Digesters

TRENCH COMPOSTING

It doesn't get more straightforward than this: Bury your scraps in a deep trench and let nature have at it. Collect scraps and add them in bulk to save you the labor of burying each banana peel individually.

Shovel

Dig holes and trenches. Scoop up browns, greens, soil, and compost . . .

Dig a trench (or hole if space is limited) with a depth of the volume of your scraps plus an additional eight inches. Drop in food scraps, mixing in a little soil to put scraps in contact with the soil ecosystem. Cover it all up with at least eight inches of soil to prevent critters from detecting the morsels below.

Use this method directly inground or in a tall raised bed that allows for eight inches of soil on top of what you bury. Rotate burial plots around your space to distribute nutrients and to allow time for previous contributions to break down.

SHEET COMPOSTING (AKA LASAGNA GARDENING)

If only there were a garden that grew lasagna. Alas, lasagna's only role here is to inspire the sheet-composting technique. The approach is simple: layer browns, greens, and finished compost or peat moss in a raised-bed-style compost casserole that, once you achieve your desired height, can be planted in directly. As the layers slowly decompose below, plants eat up the nutrients from above.

Sheet composting can be done anywhere you would put a raised bed. What's particularly fun is your raised compost bed need not conform to any particular shape, style, or size. Tall and narrow, long and wide, an elegant kidney shape—as long as it fits and looks the way you like, it's all good. Create fun borders with straw bales, cinder blocks, or bricks. Be creative with available materials.

Here's how to do sheet composting:

1. Start by placing a few inches of cardboard or newspaper on the ground. Over soil, this prevents weeds from sprouting. On concrete, it absorbs excess water.
2. Lay down 1 inch of browns; add some water.
3. Lay down 1 inch of greens; add some water.
4. Alternate layers of browns and greens, making sure your top layer is always a few inches of browns to serve as a biofilter.
5. Repeat steps 2 through 4 until your bed is full. If you're doing continuous (versus batch) composting, make sure your top layer is always several inches of browns or soil to prevent pests and odor.
6. When you've reached your desired height, it's time to plant. Top your bed off with a thick layer of finished compost and soil. Then add flowers, herbs, and shrubs to your heart's content. Make sure to plant items with shallow roots to start, as decomposition activity in lower levels may create an unstable environment for plants. Remember that as content decomposes, the volume of your bed will sink a bit, taking your layer of plants with it. To prevent this, wait until your lasagna bed has aged enough to have completed the bulk of its shrinkage.

DIGESTERS

Think of digesters as bellies in the earth that swallow up food waste and break it down into nutrients. Partially buried underground, these containers invite the soil ecosystem—but not outdoor pests—to come on in and enjoy the buffet through holes in their bottom and submerged sides.

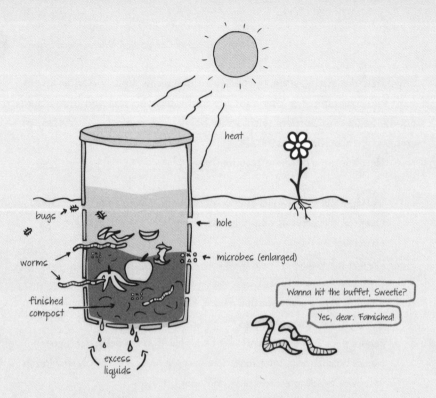

A Cross Section of a Digester at Work

Digesters come in a range of models, from basic galvanized metal trash cans drilled with holes to classy terra-cotta-style pots. Ideally, they're buried in at least half their height of soil. The exposed top absorbs sun and ambient heat, helping to warm the organics in the dark hole below. However, if your digester is buried deeper or is located in a shady space, don't worry, it will still work. It may just be a little slower.

A popular commercial digester is the aptly named Green Cone. When you open the tip of the cone and insert your greens, they fall down to the buried chamber below. For many years, the city of Seattle subsidized Green Cones for local residents and distributed more than ninety thousand of them throughout the 1990s and early 2000s, according to Carl Woestwin, who worked for Seattle Public Utilities during this period.

Bury your digester in soil with good drainage, as digesters are typically fed a diet of greens that release a lot of water as they decompose. Not sure how well drained your soil is? Cornell University recommends this method. Dig a hole twelve inches deep and fill it with water. After it drains, fill it with water again and measure the depth of the water. In fifteen minutes, measure again and multiply the amount the water has decreased by four. This tells you how much your soil drains in an hour. Good drainage is a minimum of one inch.

If you've got poor drainage, dig deeper and create a reservoir from stones where liquids can pool. Or ditch the underground concept and bury your digester in a tall raised bed instead.

Important note: Do not bury your digester below the water table in your area. A good sign you've hit it? Water pooling in the bottom of your hole as you dig. You want water flowing out of your digester, not seeping in.

Feeding your digester is a cinch: open it up, throw in your kitchen scraps, close it back up, and walk away. Microbes, worms, and insects will start working right away. As you can probably imagine, digesters have a high likelihood of going anaerobic, as you're not required to balance

Digesters stomach heavy loads of all green material.

contents with browns. If you notice unpleasant odors when you open it up and would prefer not to, top off your contribution with a layer of browns.

As for pest control, if crafty rodents, stray dogs and cats, or raccoons manage to remove the lid of your digester, put a cinder block, heavy rock, or bricks on top of it to weigh it down.

Harvesting

When your digester is full of scraps, you have two choices:

1. Stop feeding it and let nature finish breaking down the contents. Having a second digester allows you to keep composting your scraps in the meantime.

> My favorite lazy way to feed my soil is using a food digester in the middle of my garden bed. I just have this small, galvanized container with tons of holes. It's rat proof with a lid. I bury it three-quarters of the way into the garden so it doesn't stick out much and isn't too visible. And I simply put my vegetable scraps in there and keep it covered. Since it is in the middle of my garden bed, it feeds the soil food web. I don't ever harvest it. I just wait for it to sort of disappear and then I add more. It breaks down fairly quickly. I find it to be really great for people like me who are inherently lazy. It doesn't need to take a lot of time or a lot of space.
>
> **—Sheri Hinshaw,** Master Composter/
> Soil Builder Program coordinator, Seattle Tilth

2. Harvest half: Using a shovel, pitchfork, trowel, or gloved hands, remove all the unfinished material in the top layers of your digester and set them aside. Scoop out the finished material at the bottom. Replace the unfinished material and continue feeding.

Feeling handy? Cut the bottom out of a DIY digester (page 75) before you bury it. When it's full of nearly finished compost, simply pull up the digester from the hole, cover your scraps with eight inches of soil, and re-bury the digester elsewhere. In a few weeks, harvest the finished compost, or simply leave it in the ground and plant right on top of it.

DIY: DIGESTER

Journey underground with this easy-to-make digester. Galvanized metal trash cans are popular choices because the metal is good at conducting heat and they are incredibly sturdy. Popular commercial digesters are made with recycled plastics, but high-quality, food-grade plastic buckets can also get the job done.

YOU WILL NEED:

- 1 trash can or bucket with tight-fitting lid
- Drill with a minimum bit size of ¼-inch, but can be bigger; if you plan to work with metal, make sure your bit has enough bite to get through it
- Safety goggles if drilling in metal to protect from sparks and debris

MAKING THE DIGESTER:

1. Drill holes in the lower half and bottom of your container, about 3 to 4 inches apart. The number of holes you make will depend on the size of the container you're burying.
2. If you want a bottomless digester, convenient for removing the digester while leaving the compost and compostables behind in the soil where they lie,

then remove the bottom of your container. Techniques and tools required vary depending on the material your digester is made of.

3. Follow the maintenance and care instructions in the previous section.

Underground composting is an easy, fun, and out-of-sight strategy for composting. But going underground isn't the only way to keep your compost under wraps. Discreet and easy methods are also available to you indoors. The next two chapters discuss how.

6 THE WORMDERFUL WORLD OF INDOOR VERMICULTURE

"Eww."

I know.

That's how most people react when they hear the word *worms*. And I probably can't print what they say when I reveal that I live with thousands—yes, thousands—of earthworms in my Queens apartment, regularly and joyfully harvesting their poop for my plants.

As crazy as it sounds, vermicomposting, the practice of composting organic waste with earthworms, is one of the most sane, practical, and fascinating ways to make black gold. It's a particularly helpful compost system for people who lack outdoor space, or any space for that matter, because worms are a perfect, productive pet that can live in cramped indoor quarters. When corralled with greens and browns into habitats called worm bins and flow-through systems, earthworms produce a uniquely powerful product—richer, more nutritious, and packed with beneficial bacteria than what's made in wormless compost piles.

If you're still shuddering, let me assure you, I used to be one of the *"Eww"* people too. The most contact I ever had with worms before vermicomposting was stepping carefully around an occasional limp one lying shriveled on the sidewalk after a rainstorm.

I found them, to put it bluntly, slightly horrific and very much gross.

It's funny, though, how quickly *"Eww"* can turn to *"Aw"* when it comes to worms.

Earthworms carry a huge load on their little boneless backs. Out in the field and on the forest floor, they help aerate the soil, consume organic matter, and act as a living subway system that transports tons of beneficial microbes throughout the soil web.

There are several thousand species of earthworms that can be found in garden soil. They're the workhorses, or workworms, that till the land and transform dead vegetation into nutritious, healthy, bacteria-filled food for plants.

Worm poop, also called castings or vermicastings, is famously rich in nutrients and beneficial bacteria. According to the book *Teaming with Microbes* by Jeff Lowenfels and Wayne Lewis, worm castings have five times the available nitrogen, ten times the potash (an alkaline potassium compound), one and one-half times the calcium, three times the usable magnesium, and seven times the available phosphate found in non-worm-processed soil. Plus, they're 50 percent higher in organic matter than soil that hasn't passed through a worm's gut, which boosts the vital humus content we explored in chapter 1. That's a whole lotta goodness packed into that poop and a huge reason why vermicompost (compost that contains castings and other decomposed materials) tops many a gardener's list of favorite soil amendments. Just a tiny bit of vermicompost goes a long way in caring for plants and soil.

Earthworms feed on the organic matter in soil and the microorganisms that help decompose it. Surprisingly, it's the bacteria in their digestive tract, versus the worm itself, that produce the enzymes that break down the organic matter the worm has ingested. These enzymes also break down chemical bonds, making nutrients more available for plants to absorb. Because of their amazing digestive systems, worms have incredible potential to remediate polluted soil. Studies have shown that worms break down heavy metals, PCBs (or polychlorinated biphenyls, a cancer-causing compound previously used in oils and adhesives), pathogenic fungi, and other not-so-niceties in the soil.

Now, while that is well and good out on the forest floor, how does this work in the cramped studio you've *just* redecorated in impeccable Hollywood Regency decor? With the help of a tiny, ravenous, unadventurous, fast-reproducing earthworm species called *Eisenia fetida* or, more casually, the red wiggler—that's how.

GETTING TO KNOW THE RED WIGGLER

Eisenia fetida are model citizens of an indoor compost empire and a small-space composter's best friend. They can live in containers of many sizes and shapes that fit perfectly in the cubbies, cabinets, and closets of apartments, workplaces, and classrooms. Unlike the random subletter you got stuck with from Craigslist, worms make wonderful roomies. They're quiet, take up little space, and eat the food you *don't* want—not the Girl Scout cookies you clearly taped a DO NOT EAT sign on.

When provided with a balanced environment, red wigglers require very little maintenance and attention. This makes them great for passive composters, frequent travelers, or generally busy bees. On the flip side, worms don't mind frequent visits from their human overlords and are great pets for kids and curious adults. Since worms live out their whole life cycle in your worm system, you've got a front-row seat to the worm reality show: from their gestation in a tiny, lemon-shaped cocoon to a productive life eating, mating, and pooping.

Here's a peek inside this incredible creature:

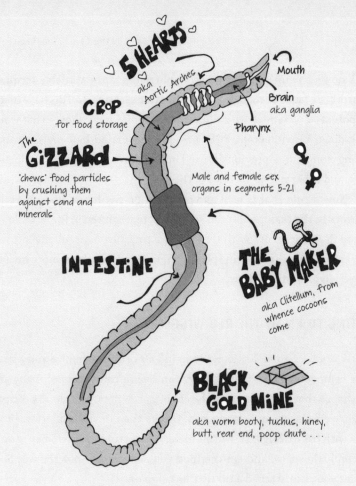

5 HEARTS
aka Aortic Arches

Mouth

Brain
aka ganglia

CROP
for food storage

Pharynx

The
GIZZARD
'chews' food particles
by crushing them
against sand and
minerals

Male and female sex
organs in segments 5-21

INTESTINE

THE BABY MAKER
aka Clitellum, from
whence cocoons
come

BLACK GOLD MINE
aka worm booty, tuchus, hiney,
butt, rear end, poop chute . . .

The Anatomy of a Worm

WHICH WORM?

Some wormers choose to vermicompost with the European night crawler, or *Eisenia hortensis,* a bigger worm that is also great as fish bait. However, Euros can be more fickle than red wigglers in terms of the conditions they thrive in. They also tend to be slower breeders, all of which make them a not-great choice for a beginner. As far as those wild worms you've seen in your backyard go—resist the temptation to add them to your bin. Largely burrowers that need lots of room to tunnel, they aren't suited for captivity and would likely die in a vermicompost bin.

Head starting to spin with earthworm wishes and vermicast dreams? To be fair, there are certain limitations to keep in mind if you choose this method of composting.

- It's a slow process that happens one tiny worm poop at a time. If you're in a rush to make mountains of compost, this may not be the method for you.
- Size matters. Each pound of worms requires a minimum of one cubic foot of space to thrive. The bigger the system you can accommodate in your home, the more worms you can have and the more scraps you can process. Plus, providing additional space gives your worm population room to grow. If you can't accommodate enough worms to consume all the scraps you create, you may need to supplement your worm bin with another form of composting.
- For better or worse, you will likely get attached to your little pets; they have a way of worming their way into your heart. If anything goes awry, you may get more emotional than if your tumbler got dry. However, you'll also likely experience a particularly strong sense of pride when you harvest their black gold, telling friends, "Look what my little darlings made!"

General Care and Maintenance for Red Wigglers

As mentioned above, red wigglers are largely housed in two different types of structures—worm bins and flow-through systems. Think of your wormery as a habitat or home to a population of very special creatures, versus that-thing-you-make-compost-in. Being mindful of the hardworking crew inside and the delicate balance of lives in the palm of your hand helps tune a wormer in to the practical essentials required for wiggler survival and care.

Many styles of bin and flow-through can be purchased premade. Or, you can make one yourself with buckets, storage totes, trash cans, or other easy-to-score items. I've even read about an experimental worm home set up in a pair of old jeans. (Yes, you read that right—jeans.) Because worms aren't particular about the space they live in, you can be creative—and space effective—about the type of home you provide them, so long as you care for them properly.

Getting Worms

Worms come by the pound (which is about a thousand worms) from specialty suppliers and cost on average about twenty-five dollars per pound. Bait shops might carry smaller amounts, but it will take longer for your population to grow big enough to make a true dent in any greens. Local vermicomposters may also share with you; I hear they're a nice bunch.

If your worms have been shipped to you, they may arrive sluggish and dried out from their travels. Consider giving your worms a few spritzes from a water bottle to rehydrate them after their journey.

Bedding

Like the luxurious down comforter you curl up under each winter, worms take refuge in billowy, bountiful bedding too. Their bedding source, however, consists entirely of browns that supply the worms (and microbes) with much-needed carbon. As with other compost systems, bedding provides a great filter for pests and odors and helps regulate moisture levels by absorbing excess liquid.

Wormeries start off packed with dampened bedding that has (you guessed it) the wet feel of Armando the Wrung-Out Sponge. In time, the bedding breaks down, just as food scraps do, and needs to be replenished.

All of the following make good bedding materials for worm bins:

- Newspaper cut into one-inch-wide strips or shredded into ribbons (avoid confetti-style shredded paper, which can clump up)
- Ripped-up cardboard egg cartons and drink trays
- Cut-up corrugated cardboard in one-inch-wide strips
- Paper towel and toilet paper rolls cut into ringlets

Note: Avoid browns with waxy or oily surfaces, such as magazines, cereal boxes, and greasy pizza boxes.

Temperature

Like most people, red wigglers are most comfortable in the 55- to 75-degree Fahrenheit range but will tolerate temps as low as 40 degrees and as high as 90 degrees. They can survive in a pH of five to nine, with the sweet spot clocking in at seven.

When choosing a location for your worm bin, make sure to keep it out of direct sunlight and away from heaters, air conditioners, and any electronics that generate temperature extremes. Worm systems may even be kept outside if they are protected from direct sunlight, rain, and wild temps.

Feeding

As with any pet, it can be so, so, tempting to keep . . . giving . . . worms . . . more . . . food (especially since you want that poop). After all, many websites and books say that red wigglers eat up to half their weight in food scraps a day. Why not keep shoveling it in?

Beware! It's an impressive factoid—and true in ideal, optimized conditions. In reality, we don't always achieve the ideal—at least not right off the bat.

Overfeeding a worm bin is one of those simple, innocent acts that cause chaos and, in the worst case, wormicide in your wormery. Because worm bins are enclosed and usually made of nonporous plastic, they tend to retain a lot of moisture. If you add more greens than the worms can consume, the scraps will start to rot, causing several unsavory conditions:

- Foul odor
- Anaerobic decomposition
- Soggy, sludgy compost
- An influx of liquid- and acid-loving pests such as mites and springtails
- Overheating
- Mass death and possible nightmares haunted by the souls of your dead worms

Before you end what you've only just begun, get to know your herd of worms and learn their feeding habits.

Portion control is a great technique to help you avoid disaster. Store your worm food in portion-sized containers and feed a full portion when the previous one is nearly gone. When starting a new system, each pound of worms can be fed about two cups (one pint) of food. I designate pint-sized plastic take-out soup containers as worm-food collection bins. When one is full, I put the lid on and follow the feeding directions below. I keep a couple containers on hand to accommodate the ebb and flow of food scraps. When it's time for a feeding, I always know I've got just the amount I need at the ready.

What do worms like to eat? Mostly raw fruit and vegetables, with the exception of citrus. Citrus is very acidic, which is not ideal for a worm habitat. Plus, the limonene found in citrus peels has been found to harm worms. If you're mad for fresh lime in your margarita, you may need an alternative system. Never add meat, dairy, cooked, or oily foods.

Here are the basic steps of feeding your worm system:

1. When your scrap collection container is full, cover it and pop it in the freezer. The arctic chill kills pest eggs that may lie on the surface of your scraps, which is a great way to deter fruit flies and other undesirables from taking up residence in your wormery.

2. When you're ready to feed your worms, take the frozen portion out and thaw it. Once it thaws, pour any excess liquid that pools at the bottom of your container down the drain. This helps keeps your system from getting too wet. (Steps 1 and 2 go a long way in pest control and maintaining moisture balance, so don't skip them.)

3. Pull away a corner of bedding and dump in your scraps. Spread them out a little so they don't compact in a ball, which can sometimes lead to anaerobic conditions or a pocket of hot compost. Cover the food with bedding and close your worm system.

4. Check back in a few days. If the food is almost entirely gone, give them another portion of the same size, close to their original feeding place so the worms don't have too far to travel. If there is still a lot of recognizable food left, do *not* add any new food. If the food has begun to rot and become unpleasant, take some out. This means the portion you provided is too big for your worms.

5. Continue to repeat steps 2–4. Soon you'll see how long it takes for the worms to complete a portion. You'll also start to see how the moisture from your scraps affects the bin. Adjust portions and establish a feeding schedule to fit your lifestyle and the worms' behavior.

WHERE THERE'S A WILL, THERE'S A WORM

In 2008 Will Allen, a former pro basketball player and the son of a sharecropper, received a MacArthur Genius Grant for his work as CEO and founder of Growing Power. Bringing healthy food education, cultivation, and distribution to underserved communities in Milwaukee and Chicago, Allen has helped countless urban gardeners of all ages build flourishing food systems.

Composting is a huge part of Allen's garden and education program, and he nurtures a particular soft spot for worms. Each year, Growing Power uses giant windrows to compost more than forty-three million pounds of food waste, much of which is sourced from businesses such as breweries and coffee shops. Allen and his team inoculate windrows with red wigglers, which happily munch away at the feast. Unfinished compost is also fed to fifty giant raised worm beds at Growing Power, where red wigglers transform it into gorgeous black gold. Utterly genius.

For more information, visit www.growingpower.org.

Harvesting

While removing compost from a worm system isn't hard or labor inten-sive, it does take a little bit of strategy. Your prized population of black-gold miners lives in the compost you covet. To keep your wormery operating at full capacity, you have to separate them from their poop.

Flow-through systems are designed to manipulate worms in a spe-cial migration pattern that, over time, leaves finished compost in an easily accessed area. Bins require a bit more finesse, as finished compost, bed-ding, fresh greens, and worms comingle in a single space. The good news is that there are very passive ways to manage both systems that require only a couple of simple steps that you'll read about in just a bit.

USING YOUR VERMICOMPOST

Worm poop potency means a little goes a long way. (Remember that crazy nutrient load discussed earlier in the chapter?) Vermicompost can be used anywhere you'd put regular compost . . . and you can use a whole lot less: a bit versus a bunch. Here are some of the ways it can be used:

- Top dress plants with an inch of vermicompost
- Mix into potting soil (ratio: 3:1 soil to vermicompost)
- Revamp lifeless soil

Another great way to use vermicompost is in an aerated worm-compost tea. Like other compost teas, aerated worm-compost tea can be poured into plant soil or sprayed on foliage. The microbially rich population of worm poop gives worm tea a particular oomph by helping plants defend against disease and unsavory elements in the soil while making nutrients more easily accessible to the soil ecosystem.

Ready to brew a gallon or two?

 DIY: AERATED WORM-COMPOST TEA

YOU WILL NEED:

- 1 vermicompost "tea bag" (basically an old nylon stocking or equivalent)
- Worm poop
- Five-gallon bucket of rainwater or a bucket of tap water that has been left to sit out overnight to dechlorinate
- 2 Tbsp unsulfured molasses
- Something to aerate the tea with, such as an aquarium air pump and air stone (which is normally used in fish bowls and tanks to circulate air in water)

MAKING THE TEA:

1. Fill the tea bag with a handful of worm poop and submerge it in the water.
2. Pour 2 tablespoons of molasses—which is a food source for the microbes in the worm poop—into the water.
3. Submerge the bubbler in the water, turn it on, and let it run for 24 to 36 hours. During this time, the air and the energy derived from the molasses will send the microbes into a wild reproductive frenzy.
4. Apply the tea directly to the soil or spray it on foliage. Use it as soon as you can after making it, because the microbe population will die off in a few days.

We sell our tea at the local farmers market, and we write on the label that it should be used within a week. There are other companies that market worm-casting teas with longer shelf life. I have used some of them, and I think they do have some benefit, there are nutrients in there, but I am skeptical about the microbial content. People go to the market to buy fresh stuff. You are not going to keep your lettuce for more than a week for the most part, and you're not going to keep your tea. You are going to buy this now and use it in your garden this week.

—**Chris Cano**, of Gainesville Compost

VERMICOMPOSTING SYSTEMS

Tending worms is a surprisingly addictive habit. It's incredible to watch the creation of compost, with creatures you can actually touch and play with. While ant farms have tunnels and, um, more tunnels (yawn), worms make magic when transforming trash to treasure. If you have kids, they will love interacting with the worms. You'll also be setting them up for a lifetime of nonsqueamish curiosity about Ma Earth and all of her creatures.

The previous sections covered the general nuts and bolts of caring for your worms. Now let's dig into the details of caring for and making the worlds they live in.

Worm Bins

THE DIRT ON WORM BINS

- Very affordable to free when you do it yourself
- Comes in a range of sizes and shapes to best accommodate small-space composters
- Requires attention to moisture balance, as they can retain a lot of water
- Low-maintenance upkeep

You know that giant tub of gummy worms from the bulk shop that you've been eating your way through on Saturday nights? Well, imagine drilling a few holes in the lid and stuffing the tub with damp shredded paper and a banana peel or two. Then imagine that all of the gummies transformed into real, live red wiggler worms. Presto! You've got a worm bin.

The concept behind worm bins is deliriously simple: Put a bunch of worms in a ventilated container. Give them food scraps and snuggly dampened bedding to live in and feed on. Store at a comfortable temperature, feed regularly, and *boom*, instant ecosystem.

Worm bins come in many forms, from tiny storage totes to outdoor wood benches. As worms move around the bin chomping scraps and bedding, they leave piles of vermicompost behind. When there's enough for you to collect and/or the inspiration hits you, harvest and enjoy.

To build your worm bin ecosystem you will need the following items:

- A place to store your worm bin out of direct sunlight and away from any temperature extremes
- Red wiggler worms
- A worm bin, either purchased or made (with one cubic foot of space for each pound of worms)
- Enough dry bedding (brown) material to fill at least two times the volume of

your bin, as the bedding will compact once you dampen it (see the list of best bedding options on page 83)

- Water in a big bowl or a spritz bottle for wetting the bedding
- One portion of worm food (greens), previously frozen, then thawed and drained of excess liquid
- A handful of finished compost (optional)

Setting Up a Worm Bin

The worms have arrived and you're a-wiggle with excitement. Whether you purchase a commercial worm bin or make your own (instructions below), setup is the same. Ready to create a home, sweet home for your new herd?

1. Dampen about 90 percent of your bedding. By dampen, I do not mean soak, drown, or flood it. Just dampen it so it feels likes Armando the Wrung-Out Sponge (he's the best!). Some people dunk all of their bedding in a bowl of water, squeeze it out, fluff it, and place it in the bin. I like to use a spritz bottle, as I find that misting is easier for controlling moisture levels.

2. Fill your worm bin with dampened bedding and place the 10 percent of dry bedding on the very top. The dry top layer serves as a moisture regulator, absorbing any excess liquid that develops in the bin below. The dry bedding won't harm your worms; they'll be happy hanging out in the damp, food-rich region below. All the bedding in your bin should be able to support a plate without packing down. If it doesn't support it, add more bedding until it does.

3. Pull back a corner of your bedding so the bottom of your bin is visible and drop in the prepared portion of worm food. If you have the optional handful of finished compost, sprinkle that on top of the scraps to introduce microbes into the food source.

4. Drop in your worms. This is the most exciting moment of starting a worm bin. Get the cameras ready, as it is an impressive sight. Dump the worms on

top of the food scraps. Once you've had your fill of ooohing, ahhhing, and gawking at the worms, cover them up with the bedding.

5. Let your worms get acclimated. New worms are sort of like kids on the first day of camp—they're a little restless and weirded out about their new surroundings. To encourage them to stay put, keep the lid off your bin and shine a bright light into it for the first night. (A regular table lamp will do just fine.) Because worms are sensitive to light, they'll hide out deep in the bedding and grow accustomed to their new home. They'll have no desire to explore. You can also just put the lid on your bin directly; just be aware that some curious escapees may flee out your ventilation holes.

6. Check in the next day. Worm population intact? Hooray! You've had your first successful night as a worm parent. If you kept the lid off, blow your little ones a kiss and put the lid on the bin.

7. In a few days, check on your worms. Do little black dots and dashes streak the sides of your bin and the bedding? That's worm Morse code for "I pooped here!" Perform the following tasks to gauge the conditions of your bin. Do this every time you open your bin to maintain bin health and prosperity.

   • Evaluate moisture levels: If there is condensation on the inner lid or walls of your bin, or if liquid is pooling at the bottom, leave the lid off so moisture can evaporate. Add dry bedding to help absorb excess moisture. The amount to add and length of time to leave the bin uncovered will be determined by how wet the environment is. Wet conditions hint either that you have fed too much food at once or that the items you picked—such as watermelon rinds—were excessively wet. If the bedding is dry to the touch throughout the bin, spritz it to restore wrung-out sponge conditions.

   • See if the worms are ready for another feeding. If most of the food from your previous feeding is gone, put a new frozen, thawed, and drained portion next to the previous one. Remember to feed under the bedding layer, which creates a filter so pests can't get in and odor can't get out. It also helps congregate the worms and their castings in one place.

- Continue adding handfuls of bedding to your bin as older bedding is consumed. Bedding can be added dry if your moisture levels are balanced or wet. Add damp bedding if the bin is dry throughout.

Note: Steps 1–3 can be prepared a few days in advance of the arrival of your worms. Some folks like to use this time to get the decomposition going and to adjust moisture levels, if needed.

Harvesting Your Worm Bin

A month or two after starting your bin, you'll notice some exciting changes taking place inside. A delicious, earthy smell will tickle your nostrils when you open it and a dark layer of rich black gold will carpet the bottom of the bin.

Woo hoo, it's time to harvest!

If you don't mind losing some of your worm herd or want to add worms to the soil you're feeding compost to, then dig down, scoop it up, and add what you've collected to your plants.

Most folks prefer to keep the worms working hard in the bin. This means making sure there are as few mature worms, baby worms, and co-coons in your harvest as possible.

The following methods will help you separate them out:

The Great Migration Method

Slow but ridiculously easy, the great migration is a method of organizing worm-bin contents so the worms separate themselves out of the finished compost. The key factor in this method is time and patience, making it perfect for the lazy wormer.

The great migration can start as soon as you see a few inches of rich, black compost lining the bottom of your bin.

For this method, it is incredibly helpful to have a hand rake. While you can do this with your hand, there's a potential muck factor that comes with rooting around the bottom of your bin.

Here's what you do:

1. Remove the bedding layer of your bin and set it aside.
2. Remove any significant portions of uneaten food from your worm bin and also set that aside.
3. Take a moment and feast your eyes on the amazing carpet of black gold you've helped create (optional, but recommended).
4. Using a hand rake, drag all of the vermicompost and any worms in it over to one side of the bin. Pile your vermicompost high; if you only have enough to fit in a corner, that's no problem.
5. "Fluff" your compost with your hand rake. This helps air it out and disturbs any pockets of worms hiding out, encouraging them to seek calmer land. If your compost is wet and mucky, this will be particularly helpful.
6. Put the bedding and uneaten food in the now-empty space adjacent to your vermicompost pile. Add more bedding, if needed, to fill up the bedding side of the bin. This is a great opportunity to regulate your moisture levels. If your compost was wet and dense, add only dry bedding on top. If the contents of your bin seemed dry, give the bedding a little spritz of water. Do not cover the separated vermicompost with bedding.
7. Resume portion feeding as usual, putting food scraps on the bedding side only. In time, worms will vacate the vermicompost and mosey over to where the food is.
8. Continue to fluff your finishing vermicompost with your hand rake periodically, as often as you feed your bin. As moisture evaporates, vermicompost turns lightweight, crumbly, and only slightly damp to the touch.
9. Wait. It may take a few weeks, maybe even months, for the cocoons in the

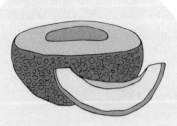

Baby worms love munching melon.

vermicompost to hatch and for all of the worms to migrate to the bedding side.

10. Eventually, fluffing reveals that the worms have vacated the compost. Hooray! It's likely most of your cocoons have hatched as well. It's time to harvest. Scoop up the compost. Use it right away, or place it in a ventilated container for a couple more weeks. During this time, the remaining cocoons will hatch. Bait the babies by placing a food scrap such as melon rind on top of the compost. Worms will gather under and on it for easy removal.

11. Fill the empty space in your bin with fresh bedding and continue caring for your worms as usual.

Make Mountains out of Worm Hills Method

If you'd prefer a more hands-on and immediate harvest, rustle up a bright light and a large, flat surface you can put vermicompost on. A tarp laid out in the sun on a mild day works nicely, but don't try this during a scorcher.

1. Remove the bedding layer of your bin and set it aside.
2. Remove any significant portions of uneaten food from your worm bin and set that aside as well.
3. Scoop the finished vermicompost and any worms in it onto your flat surface and divide it into several small mounds, at least six inches apart from each other.
4. Put the bedding and uneaten food back in the bin.
5. Add any additional fresh bedding required to fill up your bin. As mentioned in the previous method, add dry bedding if your bin contents feel wetter than Armando the Wrung-Out Sponge. If it's dry throughout, give your fresh bedding a few spritzes of water.

6. Cover your bin. You're done with it for now.

7. Shine your light on the vermicompost mounds. The worms will retreat to the center of the mounds away from the light.

8. Wait ten or fifteen minutes, then gently brush compost off the outer layer of your mounds. Collect it and put it aside. If the compost is wet and sticky, you may need to leave it out longer so upper layers have time to dry out for easy brushing.

9. Repeat step 8 until your compost has mostly been collected and all that's left are little balls of huddling worms.

10. Collect the worms and return them to the bin. Resume regular care and maintenance.

11. Use your vermicompost immediately, or if you'd like to make sure all cocoons present have hatched, let your compost sit in a ventilated container for a few weeks. Fluff it with your garden fork if it's very wet. The cocoons will hatch and the baby worms will grow. To remove them from your finished compost, bait them with melon rind or other green on the top of the finished compost. The baby worms will congregate at the food source, and you can scoop 'em out.

 ### DIY: SIMPLE WORM BIN

Red wigglers are very adaptable creatures and can live in a wide range of containers. I've made worm bins out of everything from old storage bins to a bear-shaped plastic container that was once home to animal crackers. As long as worms have adequate ventilation, and their browns, greens, and moisture levels are kept balanced, they'll be happy and prolific.

YOU WILL NEED:

- Storage bin that provides 1 cubic foot of space per 1 pound of worms you plan to house. If this is your first stab at vermicomposting, I recommend going with a standard square or rectangular storage tote and leave the experimental bear shapes for when you have a little more experience. Scale the size up or down as needed to accommodate the number of worms you buy.

- Drill with a ¼-inch drill bit, or similar size
  (*Note*: Some inexpensive, brittle plastics crack under the pressure of a drill, so choose your bin with care.)

BUILDING THE BIN:

These instructions are for a ten-gallon storage tote but can be sized up or down as needed. A ten-gallon tote is a perfect starter size for one pound of worms, providing plenty of room for them to grow.

1. Drill ventilation holes in the lid, spaced a few inches apart.
2. Drill holes around the top perimeter of the bin, also spaced every few inches.
3. Add the bedding, worms, and feedstock, and care for your worms according to the instructions above.

DIY Worm Bin

Home sweet home, for thousands of red wigglers.

Tip: If your DIY bin begins to collect condensation on the top, either you are adding too many greens or there isn't enough ventilation in the bin. Drill more air holes and monitor your system.

Tip: If your bin is always dry and you are super-duper sure you're adding the appropriate amount of browns and greens, you may have too many air holes. Grab some duct tape and seal some of the ventilation holes from the inside of your bin, sticky side facing out.

THE FLOW-THROUGH SYSTEM

THE DIRT ON FLOW-THROUGH SYSTEMS

- Designed for easy harvesting
- Low-maintenance upkeep

Flow-through worm systems rely on brute tummy logic. Since red wigglers migrate to food sources, these systems lure worms up (in a vertical system) or over (in a horizontal one) with fresh feedings. Once they've eaten everything they can in a given place, they wiggle their way over to their next meal, leaving their castings behind for easy pickings.

Some systems are a single chamber that houses worms, bedding, and food in one place. Finished vermicompost is harvested directly from an opening at the bottom. That may be a drawstring closure on a cloth-bag system or a series of harvesting rods that agitate compost into a container below. This style of flow-through is typically handmade for the home composter, not purchased. Retail versions serve large-scale operations.

A popular version of the flow-through system uses stacked trays with mesh bottoms. As worms finish one tray of food, a new one is added on top. Worms migrate to upper trays for fresh chow, leaving castings below in trays that are easily removed for harvest. The following care directions apply to stacked-tray systems, which are pretty universal in design and care. I've included a few notes on single-chamber systems where applicable. Unfortunately, the vast array of designs makes it challenging to provide a set of universal instructions for them.

Setting Up a Flow-Through System

- Place your flow-through system in an area out of direct sunlight and away from any temperature extremes.

- If you are using a stacked-tray system, fill the first tray with bedding and dampen it so the bedding feels like Armando the Wrung-Out Sponge.
- If you are using a single-chamber flow-through, place a few sheets of newspaper along the bottom, then add several inches of dampened bedding.
- Some commercial versions such as the WormFactory 360 and Can-O-Worms come with their own set-up instructions.

General Feeding for a Flow-Through System

Because more air circulates in a flow-through system, flow-throughs can be a little more forgiving in terms of feedings. Increased air means less chance of unpleasant, wet pockets forming, as the breeze distributes moisture throughout the system and out of it. Some highly successful commercial products say you can feed on a 1:1 brown-to-green ratio, unlike the 2:1 common to other systems.

Feeding a flow-through system is basically creating a journey from point A to point B. Add a portion of food to starting point A. Each subsequent feeding brings the worms closer to point B, which is the next tray in a stacked system or the top of your single-chamber unit. As worms get closer to point B, they leave rich vermicompost in their wake for easy harvest at point A.

As always, start adding food conservatively and give yourself a few weeks to get to know the eating habits of your worms.

There are two ways to harvest a finished tray:

1. In the first method, dump out the finished compost and add the now-empty tray to the top of the system with fresh food and bedding. To rescue stragglers from the finished compost, poke around and pick them out by hand or bait them with a juicy rind like melon. In a day or so, any remaining worms will converge under the food for easy pickings.
2. Alternatively, remove the bottom tray and place it in the top position. Make sure the tray's mesh bottom is in contact with the contents of the tray below.

Flow-Through Stacked Tray Worm System

Clockwise:

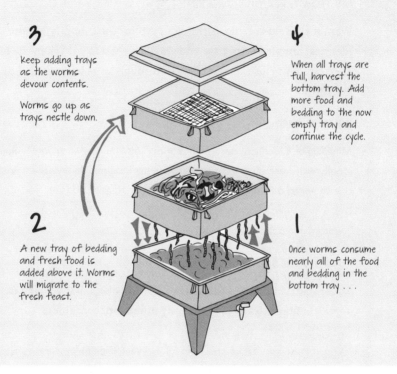

3

Keep adding trays as the worms devour contents.

Worms go up as trays nestle down.

4

When all trays are full, harvest the bottom tray. Add more food and bedding to the now empty tray and continue the cycle.

2

A new tray of bedding and fresh food is added above it. Worms will migrate to the fresh feast.

1

Once worms consume nearly all of the food and bedding in the bottom tray . . .

Shine a bright light into the top tray and rake through its contents with a hand rake. Lingering worms will take cover from the light and commotion in the dark, calm trays below.

Maintenance

Managing flow-through systems is a bit different from managing worm bins because a lot more air tends to circulate through them. Overly dry conditions are more of a threat than overly wet ones, as moisture continually evaporates into thin air. You may need to spritz your system occasionally if it's too dry.

DIY: FLOW-THROUGH WORM BIN

Want a stacked-tray flow-through system? Just modify a bunch of identical Simple Worm Bins and you'll be good to go! When the bins are nested, worms migrate upward through large holes drilled in all but the bottom bin.

YOU WILL NEED:

- Minimum of 3 identical storage bins or buckets that nest within each other, ideally with some room to spare between the bottoms when stacked. Each one serves as a "tray" in your stacked system.
- Drill with a ¼-inch and ½-inch drill bit
- 1 storage bin or bucket lid

BUILDING THE BIN:

These instructions use three five-gallon buckets, but you can easily adapt the steps to any type and any number of containers.

1. Using your ¼-inch drill bit, drill a handful of ventilation holes in the lid and around the upper perimeter of each bucket every few inches apart.
2. Using the bigger bit, drill migration holes for worms in the bottoms of two nesting buckets. Place holes about 2 inches apart. The third bucket is the bottom bucket and should not have migration holes.
3. Start your worm bin in the bottom bucket with the instructions on page 89. Put the lid on.
4. Feed and care for the bucket like a normal worm bin until you have several inches of nearly finished vermicompost at the bottom.
5. Remove all the bedding from the bottom bucket and place nesting bucket 1 within it. The migration holes should be in direct contact with the layer of vermicompost and any remaining food scraps in the bottom bucket. If the

compost and food layer isn't high enough to reach the bottom of the nested bucket, return the bedding and continue tending until it is.

6. Put a layer of food scraps on the bottom of nesting bucket 1. Place all the bedding that you removed from the bottom bucket into the nesting bucket, covering the scraps. Add any additional bedding you may need so nesting bucket 1 is packed to the top with bedding. If the bedding you moved over from the bottom bucket was damp, the new bedding can be dry. Put on the lid.

7. Repeat steps 4–6, adding nesting buckets as needed. Depending on how many worms you have in your system, what you feed them, ambient environmental conditions, and the type of buckets or totes you use, this can take weeks or months.

8. When all of your nesting buckets are in the system and the topmost bucket has several inches of compost in it, harvest the compost from the bottom bucket. Nearly all of the worms should have migrated to upper buckets, including babies hatched from cocoons, leaving fluffy, finished castings behind. If you see any stragglers, pick them out and add them to bucket.

9. Move the compost from nesting bucket 1 into the bottom bucket, readying it for the next harvest. Nesting bucket 2 will now move in nesting bucket 1's slot.

10. Place the newly emptied nesting bucket 1 in the top slot, making it the new nesting bucket 2.

In a three-bucket system the bottom bucket always stays in place, housing the oldest, most finished and worm-free compost. Buckets 1 and 2 switch places . . . forever.

Tip: If you find your system is getting excessively wet but you are sure your browns and greens are balanced, try one of three things:

- Take the lid off your system to air it out.
- Drill more ventilation holes throughout your buckets.

- Drill migration holes in the bottom bucket, allowing excess water to drip out the bottom. Place your buckets in a tray to collect liquids. Propping the bucket system on bricks or old tiles will also increase airflow, systemwide. If you take this route, abandon the instructions above regarding the holeless bottom bucket and always harvest compost from the bottommost bucket. A few worms may escape out the bottom and into your catch tray, but most will be in upper buckets pigging out on the buffet.

Is it incredibly dry when you check on your worms? If so, spritz some water in your bin and/or cover a few ventilation holes with duct tape from the inside, sticky side facing out.

GENERAL TROUBLESHOOTING FOR WORM SYSTEMS

Just because you're perfect doesn't mean the conditions in your wormery will be. All sorts of drama can ensue in a worm bin. As landlord, super, and parent to your herd, it's up to you to figure out what's going wrong and correct it.

Climate Control for Your Worm System

While not as fickle as Goldilocks, red wigglers prefer it not too hot, not too cold, and juuust right. Regardless of what kind of system you choose, your worms have basic requirements to thrive. If local temps or that broken radiator create crazy conditions in the wormisphere, worm populations can suffer. They'll either flee for greener pastures or kick the bucket. Here are ways to help keep things calm.

It's Too Hot

If summer's a-blazing and your air conditioning is on the fritz, or an excess of greens is causing your bin to heat up, there's a good chance that over-warm worms are gonna head for the hills, and by hills, I mean your hard-wood floor. Avoid an afternoon of cleaning up crispy, dried worms by heeding the following advice.

- If ambient temps are the problem, cool off the bin by removing the lid and/or temporarily relocating it to a cool basement or a friend's air-conditioned pad. If relocation is impossible, lay a bottle of frozen water or ice pack in the bin to cool down ambient temps. A little bit of ice isn't strong enough to freeze the worms, so don't worry about creating wormsicles. You may, however, wish to wrap your cold pack in dry bedding, as condensation may collect on the sides, adding excess moisture to your bin.
- Did a pocket of greens start to heat up? Remove the excess greens and allow your bin to normalize. Don't feed again until all the remaining food scraps in your wormery are gone.

It's Too Cold

Worms slow down as temperatures drop, and they start to die off in freezing temps. Don't leave your babies stranded in the cold! If your worms live in a chilly space like a garage, or your apartment heater is busted, take these precautions:

- Move them. For the coldest stretches, bring them to a warm location in your home. Extreme temps should be the exception if you have a no-worms-in-house rule, lest you lose the entire population!
- Insulate the bin, being careful not to obstruct ventilation holes. Loosely toss a blanket over your wormery to protect it from a draft or cut Styrofoam "armor" to encase your worms. This will help maintain any heat generated in the bin and provide a buffer to the cold. Leave room around ventilation holes so as not to block off all airflow.
- Turn up the heat. Small-animal heating pads or a small fishbowl heater submerged in a sealed bottle of water can be put on a timer and placed

directly in your bin. If you'd prefer to heat the room (and reap some of the benefits yourself), space heaters or lamps with heat-generating lightbulbs will do the trick. When applying heat to your bin, make sure to check in every few hours to make sure you aren't overheating the worms.

It's Too Wet

Just because they're slimy doesn't mean worms like it soggy. To dry out your drippy state of affairs, try some or all of the following:

- Add more dry bedding.
- Stop feeding high-moisture foods.
- Keep the lid off for a few hours or days, as needed, so bedding can dry out.
- "Fluff" some of the compacted, wet bedding in the soggiest corners with a hand rake, to circulate air through it.

It's Too Dry

If the bedding is dry throughout your wormery and your compost is crispy or caked, supply your worms with a little liquid lunch. Spritz your bin with water until the bedding and compost feel like Armando the Wrung-Out Sponge. It's possible you're underfeeding your worms or feeding them scraps that don't supply enough moisture to the environment, such as carrot nubs and avocado peels. It's also possible that your system has too much ventilation. Tape up a few of the ventilation holes, add water when feeding, or choose wetter scraps.

The Worm Habitat Ecosystem

There goes the neighborhood. What was once a tranquil landscape of shredded paper, disappearing food scraps, and frolicking red wigglers now has little brown dots, bouncing white flecks, and some many-legged creatures cruising the scene. Looks like you've got squatters. Each one is there because conditions have shifted in your bin, making it hospitable to more than the worm population you intended. While it's rare that guest populations attack or harm worms, it's possible that in time the shifting environment that gave rise to the newcomers will. They might also compete with your worms for food.

What are these visitors, why are they there, and how do you get rid of them?

Anaerobic Microbes

Symptoms: Got a nose full of ammonia when you opened your bin? Sounds like an excess of greens got compacted and began decomposing anaerobically.

Treatment: Remove all but a practical portion of what your worms will consume and spread the remaining scraps throughout the bin so they don't clump up. Use your garden fork to fluff out and aerate the compacted compost. Then add dry browns right on top of your food scraps. If your bin is very wet at the bottom, leave the lid off to air it out.

Molds and Fungi

Symptoms: Fuzzy, colorful splotches of mold and fungus have bloomed in your worm bin like an exhibit of modern microbe art.

Treatment: These microorganisms love mellow, stagnant environments and lots of decaying matter. If you've got a bloom, it likely means there's too much food in your bin and the worms aren't eating it fast enough. Remove excess food and slow your feeding rate. The mold will disappear as its food supply does.

Potworms

Symptoms: Tiny, hair-like white worms just a few millimeters long line food scraps and the sides of your system.

Treatment: Often mistaken for baby red wigglers, potworms are

quarter-inch crawlies that proliferate in wet, acidic environments. Air out the bin, add dry bedding, and avoid adding acidic scraps such as tomatoes or kiwi to your bin until balance is restored.

GOT ACID?

As you'll recall, worms prefer a neutral pH range but can survive conditions as acidic as pH 5. As you add acidic scraps like the ones mentioned above to your worm system, the environment's acidity level moves further away from the worms' ideal and new acid-loving creatures move in. If your bin is getting acidic, try adding crushed eggshells. They are jam-packed with calcium, which is an alkaline substance that can help balance acidity.

Mites

Symptom: A sea of tiny red-brown or white dots cover food scraps.

Treatment: Mites love wet conditions; if they're around, it means your bin's getting soggy. Add dry bedding and air out the bin. Reduce the existing mite population by removing the scraps most covered with them. Bait the remaining mites with bread or melon rind until the population subsides.

Springtails

Symptom: Little white dots effervesce throughout your worm bin like little buggy bubbles of champagne.

Treatment: Called springtails, these mostly white, wingless insects have a prong on their underside that pops them into the air. They feed on mold and decaying matter and love wet conditions. Add dry bedding and air out the existing contents to get rid of them.

Fruit Flies and Fungus Gnats

Symptom: Small black and/or brown flies have taken up residence in your

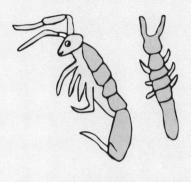

Springtails

Boinggg! Sprigtails like jumping.

Mites

Mites are kind of cute . . .
except they're not.

worm system and in the surrounding areas, dive bombing your face and sunbathing on your windows.

Treatment: Chubby brown fruit flies and sleek black fungus gnats can be seriously annoying airborne inconveniences. The best way to battle them is prevention. Freezing your scraps before a feeding kills any pest eggs that might be on fruit skins. Also, always bury your scraps under the bedding layer. This blocks flies from getting to the food layers below where they typically like to feed, reproduce, and proliferate.

If you do all of this and still find yourself with a faceful of flying devils, here's how to clear the skies:

1. Set them free: Bring your bin outside and release the teeming hoard. Make sure to shake out the bedding to agitate stragglers. Reducing the active adult population in your bin and living space will help clear the air and diminish the numbers reproducing in your bin. If you can't bring your system outside, try this beside a fully open window during daylight hours.

Inexpensive and Easy Fungus Gnat and Fruit Fly Traps

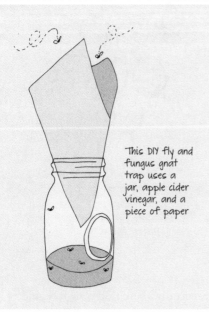

This DIY fly and fungus gnat trap uses a jar, apple cider vinegar, and a piece of paper

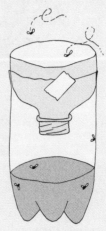

For this DIY fruit fly and fungus gnat trap all you need is a plastic beverage bottle, apple cider vinegar, a piece of tape and scissors

2. Trap them: Hang fly strips from the ceiling or stick clear ones on your windows. Flies and gnats gravitate to the light and will often congregate where it's brightest. Apple cider vinegar traps also do the trick. Flies and gnats are attracted to the scent of vinegar. With the traps described below, they fly through a funnel and can't find their way back out. When they land on the surface of the vinegar, they drown. Make your own DIY vinegar traps—it's easy!

   a. Pour apple cider vinegar into a jar and squeeze a drop of dish soap into it to break the surface tension. Curl a piece of paper into a funnel and insert the narrow end into the jar. If the funnel unfurls, secure it with a piece of tape.

   b. Cut the top off a plastic beverage bottle. Turn it upside down and insert the top into the bottom half, so the mouthpiece points down, creating a funnel. Pour in some apple cider vinegar and a drop of dish soap. Tape the two pieces together to secure them.

Weird Worm Behavior Explained

During visits to your wormery, you've noticed the natives doing a bit more than crawling around and snacking. Before you send out an APB to apprehend these deviants, find out what's really going on.

Stuck Together in Pairs

If you see two worms doing the double helix don't spoil the mood by tearing them apart—those worms are mating. Worms are hermaphrodites, meaning they have both male and female sex organs. While they can't fertilize themselves, they can simultaneously fertilize each other by snuggling up in creative spooning. A cocoon forms in the worm's clitellum (that turtleneck-looking part of their body) and slides up and off the worm's body. At first it looks like a tiny little lemon. It darkens as it ages. Cocoons house up to ten fertilized eggs, though usually only a couple hatch.

Privacy, please! Worms reproducing . . .

Climbing the Walls of Your Worm System

No, it's not you that's driving them up the walls of their wormery. It's more likely one of two things. The first may be inhospitable, extreme conditions. If things are going downhill in the bin, they're gonna run . . . er, squirm away. Refer to the climate control and pest sections for strategies on how to correct the problem.

The second reason worms climb up the walls is the weather. When a storm's brewing or there are other bumps in barometric pressure, worms tend to leave their comfortable compost or soil habitats and wander around. Experts believe this may be because of their desire to explore the surface when it's wet outside; the environment is otherwise too dry and bright on a warm, sunny day. If the weather's experiencing a twinge, don't worry; your worms will be fine and probably won't leave the system. If you find that a couple have escaped, try taking the lid off your bin and shining a bright light inside until the worms retreat back into their home.

Did It Just Pee on Me?!

There's a moment in every wormer's life when he or she finally gets a squeamish friend to hold a worm—only to have it secrete a bright yellow liquid on the person's palm. The friend starts freaking out because he's convinced the worm just peed on him (forget the fact that the worm just came out of a container full of its own poop). Soothe his fears by assuring him this liquid is coelomic fluid. The yellow liquid is released in times of stress to moisten the worm's body. Both light and the dry surface of human skin freak the worm out, so it creates the fluid to be more comfortable. Minimize worm stress by periodically spritzing them with water as you handle them.

Escapees!

Runaways are common when you first introduce worms to a new habitat or when their environment becomes inhospitable. Depending on how quickly you spot the exodus, you may be able to save some of the worms who've gotten out. Then turn your attention to saving what worms might be left inside. Why do you think they fled? Moisture or temperature extremes will usually be the culprit. Use the techniques described earlier in the chapter to mellow your system out and reestablish a stable environment.

Worm Ball

When I am stressed out, I usually isolate myself with potato chips and re-runs of television crime shows. When worms are stressed out, they clump together in balls. Reasons for stress include temperature extremes, introduction to new environments, and volatile environments. While you don't have to give each one a massage, massaging their environment can go a long way toward mellowing them out.

No Worms

If you can't find any worms in your bin, it's likely that they took one last wiggle to the big dirt pile in the sky. Worm loss can evoke strong feelings in a worm caretaker, from failure to disbelief, denial, and grief. However, all may not be lost. Worms have a strange doomsday second sense and reproduce like mad right before an untimely apocalypse, hoping their offspring will hatch during better times. Rather than toss out the contents of your system, try to diagnose and correct what went wrong. If you can restore the balance, cocoons may hatch and give you a second chance.

Charles Darwin famously wrote, "It may be doubted whether there are many other animals which have played so important a part in the history of the world as these lowly organised creatures." Aside from the "lowly" part, he was spot-on. As you get to know your worm herd, take time to appreciate their efforts and have fun with them . . . and watch the history of the world unfold right in your home.

7 BOKASHI FERMENTATION

Here's a pickle you'll want to get into.

For centuries, people have fermented food to preserve it, transform it, and cultivate the beneficial microbial cultures that do a body good. Yogurt, kimchi, and sauerkraut are just a few of the tasty delights that result from this ancient process, which goes back thousands of years. (It's also how grape juice becomes wine, which, as far as I am concerned, gives fermentation miracle status.)

Fermentation is also a great way to turn food scraps into pathogen-safe, nutrient- and microbe-rich organic matter that breaks down into a luscious soil amendment. If you've got a corner, closet, or cabinet where you can stick an airtight bucket, you've got room to ferment your food waste. If you've got a yard, raised bed, or containers of soil, you can bury your bokashi and make super soil.

Commonly known as the practice of *bokashi,* a Japanese word that means "fermented organic matter," this low-maintenance practice is easy to do and doesn't discriminate. Meat, dairy, bones, and oily and cooked foods—even the strange, viscous potions lining your condiment shelf—can all be fermented, giving a green light to food categories usually verboten in most compost piles.

Traditional food fermentation occurs in anaerobic conditions, meaning all the magic happens in the absence of air. The process goes something like this: Special bacteria, sometimes aided by yeasts and molds, are placed in an airtight container of food. (Since the key players come from the *Lactobacillus* genus of bacteria, this process is often called lacto-fermentation, or lactic-acid fermentation.) The microbes feast and party, creating by-products such as acids that ferment and preserve the food. Ta-da! Instant, long-lasting deliciousness.

The bokashi method follows the same logic. Food scraps are layered with carefully selected anaerobic microbes in an airtight bucket. The materials sit for a minimum of two weeks while you go about your business and the microbes go about theirs, breaking down odor, pathogens, and complex cellular structures. The resulting fermented food waste is soft, pliable, and rich with beneficial microbes. Once buried in an outdoor or container soil ecosystem, it

Bokashi-Friendly Foods

Dairy

Oils

Cooked Foods

Bokashi doesn't discriminate!

completes its transformation into rich, nutritious plant food. You can plant directly on top of it in just a few weeks. Or, dig it up and spread it around for use as compost in other planting beds.

Note: Some people and marketers refer to the process of fermenting food waste as "bokashi composting," which is a bit misleading. Fermenting food scraps is only the first step in making organic nutrients available to the soil. It is not the end game in your compost adventure, as your fermented scraps will still need contact with a soil or compost ecosystem before plants can enjoy the benefit. If it helps, think of bokashi as *precomposting* versus composting itself.

Sound easy? It is!

THE DIRT ON BOKASHI FERMENTATION

- Good for omnivores that want to compost meat, dairy, and cooked foods in addition to fruit and vegetable scraps.
- Low-maintenance option for those not interested in balancing carbon and nitrogen (that is: browns + greens = annoying).
- Great for handling food waste in limited space or indoors.
- Produces a liquid by-product called bokashi juice that many use to clear pipes, aid septic systems, and when diluted, feed plants.
- Fermented food scraps require burial in soil or in a composting system to complete their transformation into rich earth. If you do not have a place you can bury fermented scraps at home, this system will not work for you.

In addition to the convenience of processing any kind of scrap indoors, bokashi has a host of other perks. It's impossible for pathogens to survive the acidic environment created by fermentation, and common compost pile pests such as rats aren't big fans either. More water and nutrients are retained during the process than during aerobic composting, which means bonus goodness for the soil it's eventually buried in.

At the heart of bokashi are three families of microbes that work cooperatively to ferment food and render it safe for composting:

1. Lactic acid bacteria. Found in foods such as sauerkraut, pickles, and yogurt, it drops the pH of bucket contents, making it inhospitable for methane-producing anaerobic microbes and other unwanted pathogens.
2. Yeasts. Known best for their role in making breads and beers, yeasts break down sugars and produce vitamins, hormones, and amino acids that are consumed by fellow microbes, soil organisms, and plants.
3. Phototrophic bacteria. These powerhouses decompose organic matter and contribute to metabolic systems, helping yeasts and lactic acid bacteria work together while detoxifying their environment.

This powerful threesome was discovered quite by accident when a Japanese agricultural scholar named Dr. Teruo Higa tossed some test microorganisms into grass and soil with an astoundingly verdant effect. Over several years and additional research, he fine-tuned the microbial recipe and identified powerful microbial consortiums he dubbed "effective microorganisms," or EM for short. These collections of nonpathogenic microbes were bred in liquid serums and put on the retail market. EM is used to inoculate materials used in bokashi and in a surprising range of other ways.

When added to septic systems, the microbes help consume sludge, reduce odor, and maintain conditions. Spraying EM on surfaces with animal poop such as dog runs and livestock pens can reduce odor, decrease pest populations, and improve sanitary health. It's also fed to pets and livestock to improve digestion and health. Some human fans have mastered a microbe-based mixology that ferments EM in beverages with ingredients like pineapple and garlic. Bottoms up!

HAVE A BALL PURIFYING WATER

When activated EM, bokashi, and soil are rolled together and dried, the result is a very flingable microbe-filled mud ball that is believed to eat sludge, break down toxins, and improve water health. In fact, in 2009 eighteen thousand people in Penang, Malaysia, gathered to throw 1.2 million mud balls into a polluted river in an event called One Million Apologies to Mother Earth.

 GETTING STARTED WITH BOKASHI

The fermentation of food waste occurs in airtight buckets. Bokashi buckets are readily available for purchase and are also easy to make yourself. Most commercial buckets come in a five-gallon size. When you make your own, you can choose a size that best suits your waste stream. As long as the container is airtight, you're in good shape.

YOU WILL NEED:

- Bokashi bucket with airtight lid, drainage optional: Depending on what you put in it, a bucket full of bokashi scraps can release a lot of liquid. Some people prefer systems with a reservoir at the bottom to collect and dispose of what's often referred to as bokashi juice (do not drink it— really). Others pad a drainless bucket with paper products, stale breads, and other absorbent compostable material. Both approaches work, and instructions are provided for each method below.
- Plastic bag: Any old shopping bag will do, as long as it is bigger than the opening of your bucket when laid flat.
- Material inoculated with beneficial microbes: You can buy material already inoculated with bokashi microbes, or you can make them yourself with

EM-1. (DIY instructions on page 132.) Wheat bran is a favorite inoculant for bokashi because it's inexpensive and easy to disseminate. For this reason, many refer to inoculant as bokashi bran. However, several materials do the job beautifully, including crumbled dry leaves, coffee chaff, and sawdust. For this reason, I like to refer to inoculated material as bokashi flakes versus bokashi bran, as they sprinkle over food scraps like a fine, microbe-filled snow.

READY, SET, BOKASHI!

You've got your airtight bucket, a bagful of bokashi flakes, and a mountain of food scraps ready to go. It's time to start fermenting.

Fill Your Bucket

The key to having a good fermentation experience is making sure you create conditions that will be utterly irresistible to the microbes in play. If you lapse in bucket care, scraps—and the fluids they generate—can putrefy, transforming your bucket into the angry bowels of Mordor. (Not a Tolkien fan? Suffice to say, it's bad.) Don't let it happen to you.

Step 1

Sprinkle bokashi flakes on the bottom of your bucket. Be generous. If you can't see most of the surface of your bucket bottom, you're in good shape.

Drainless bucketeers. Add a few inches of dry, shredded, non-waxy paper or cardboard, stale bread, egg cartons, paper towel rolls, or the like to the bottom of your bucket before sprinkling a layer of bokashi flakes over it.

Step 2

Add a layer of food waste, not to exceed 2 inches. If you add too much food waste at once, your scraps won't all have access to the microbes in the bokashi flakes. If a pocket of food waste begins decomposing anaerobically with naturally occurring nonbokashi microbes, the scraps may putrefy instead of ferment.

Step 3

Sprinkle a layer of bokashi flakes over the scraps. Make sure they are well covered.

- Meats, cooked foods, and stinky, moldy mysteries from the back of your fridge require microbial reinforcements. Coat them generously with extra bokashi flakes. Don't cheap out . . . your nose will hate you for it later.
- Because putrefied meat is no joke, consider mixing meat offerings with sugar-rich scraps before adding them to the bucket. Stale cake, fruit peels, jams and jellies will give microbes the extra energy they need to power through leftover pork chops.

Step 4

Repeat steps 2 and 3 until all of the scraps you've collected for this deposit have been added.

Drainless bucketeers. Be sure to add layers of dry materials as you go to absorb the liquids that leach out of the scraps.

Step 5

Sprinkle a final layer of bokashi flakes on top of your food scraps.

Step 6

Create a bag barrier. Cover your scraps with a plastic bag and press down to squeeze out all the air hidden between the layers of food below. Tuck the bag in along the edges of the bucket, making a barrier between the scraps and any air in the remaining bucket space.

Anatomy of a Bokashi Bucket

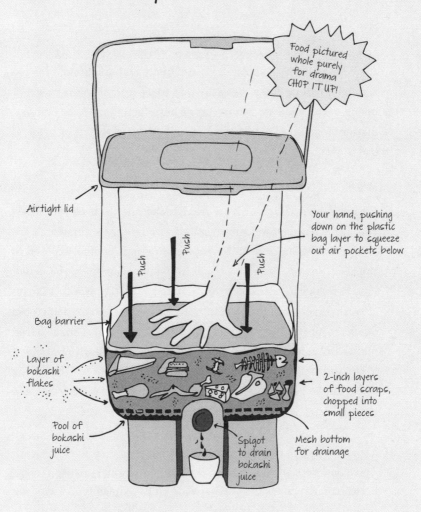

Food pictured whole purely for drama CHOP IT UP!

Airtight lid

Your hand, pushing down on the plastic bag layer to squeeze out air pockets below

Push   Push   Push

Bag barrier

Layer of bokashi flakes

2-inch layers of food scraps, chopped into small pieces

Pool of bokashi juice

Spigot to drain bokashi juice

Mesh bottom for drainage

Drainless bucketeers. If you see or feel liquids oozing up while you compress your scraps, that's a nudge to remove the bag, add another layer of dry materials and bokashi flakes, and repeat step 6.

Step 7

Seal your airtight lid completely. Don't take the resounding snap of the lid as proof it's completely closed. Run your hand around the perimeter, pressing down the entire way, to be sure. Even the tiniest of openings can allow air to creep in and putrefaction to ensue. Congratulations—you just made your first bokashi bucket deposit! Not so bad, right?

Step 8

If you selected a bucket with a drain, make sure to check your reservoir every few days and empty out any liquid that accumulates. Allowing bokashi juice to sit for extended periods of time exposed to the air in the reservoir may result in the putrefaction of the liquid. Pour the bokashi juice down the drain to see Mother Nature's Drano at work. (Ever since I started sending the gunk-chomping microbes down my pipes, I haven't had a slow drain or clog!) You can also feed plants and soil with it when you dilute bokashi juice with water at a minimum ratio of 1 part bokashi juice, 100 parts water. (The juice is too acidic to be used directly.) The color and odor of your bokashi juice will vary with the contents of your bucket.

Step 9

Add a new deposit of scraps. There may be a few days or even weeks between scrap deposits. It all depends on how much food waste you produce and how often you visit your bucket. Regardless of your deposit schedule, try to minimize the bucket contents' exposure to air. Collect scraps throughout the day, or even week, in a container you keep refrigerated until you're ready to add it. Open your bucket once a day at most.

Look inside your bucket and peel away the plastic-bag barrier.

If everything has gone to plan, your food scraps may have white mold growing on them (a good thing), and you'll catch a whiff of something pickley, like apple cider vinegar. Repeat steps 2 through 7 until your bucket is completely full.

Got blue, green, black, or Technicolor rainbow mold? Something has gone amiss, and you've cultivated microbes you don't want. Bury your bucket contents in a soil ecosystem immediately (see about burying bokashi below), making sure to add additional bokashi flakes before you cover them. This fermentation was unsuccessful. Or throw the bucket contents in the trash and start anew.

Step 10

Wait. It will take a minimum of two weeks for your scraps to finish fermenting. Temperature, moisture levels, and contents of the bucket all affect how long it will take.

Don't stop the bokashi train. A second bokashi bucket can be handy during this time, so you can continue to ferment scraps while your first bucket finishes.

Bring in da Funk
(aka, the Real Deal on Bokashi Odors)

When reading about or shopping for bokashi products online, you may see claims that this process is "utterly odorless" and "won't stink up your home." Sound a bit too good to be true? You've hit it right on the nose.

Because food-waste fermentation occurs in an airtight bucket, it's fair to say that the bokashi process is odorless . . . when the bucket is closed. When the fermented food-waste scraps are eventually buried under a thick layer of soil, the final stages of composting also don't smell.

However, it's a different story when bucket contents are exposed. A well-maintained bucket will smell lightly of pickles and vinegar. A poorly maintained bucket can evoke anything from eau de trash heap to eau de AH OMG HELP. In either case, you and/or surrounding noses may find the odors unpleasant.

There are four scenarios during food-scrap fermentation where you'll cross paths with odors.

Fermenting food scraps

As your food scraps ferment, they create lactic acids that, in general, give off a pickled or vinegary smell. Depending on what types of organic material you put in your bucket, this scent can vary, and it's safe to say you'll never get the exact same smell twice. Every time you open the bucket to add more scraps, or as you transfer your completely fermented scraps to the soil to complete composting, you'll catch a whiff of science at work. This smell may also spread into the immediate vicinity or get onto your hands if you touch the scraps directly. Once you close the bucket, the smell may hover a few minutes but eventually dissipates. Opening your bucket outside or by open windows can help to prevent the smell from lingering.

Rotting food scraps

When good fermentation goes bad to the bones, meat, and other goodies that you've put in your bucket, you'll learn what puts the *pee-eww* in putrefaction. Rotten food smells like, well, rotten food, and you may discover parts of your bucket have gone bad when you open it or when you dump your scraps into the soil to break down. Follow the best practices outlined on pages 116 to 121, to avoid an olfactory crisis. Knowing it's a possibility should be enough to make sure you do it right.

Bokashi juice

When you drain your bokashi bucket of its juice, you'll get a whiff of the by-product of the fermentation process. This juice can range from a light vinegar smell to a complex brew of the items you've packed in there (including those fish heads and that chicken fat)—but pickled. Again, you smell this only in the moments it is exposed to air. Once it goes down the drain, it's mostly gone. If the smell lingers in the pipes, run the tap to wash it down. You won't wash away all the microbes or their benefit.

Composting fermented scraps indoors

If you bury bokashi scraps outside, you won't encounter odor. Even if you turn it and cover it over again, any lingering smells dissipate up to the sky. However, if you bury your scraps in a storage tote of soil or worm bin and you work with it indoors, there's a good chance the pickle smell may waft into the surrounding area when exposed.

ANAEROBIC DIGESTERS

Often, *anaerobic* is a bad word when it comes to dealing with organic wastes. In the world of composting, anaerobic conditions create methane and ammonia. If this occurs accidentally in an aerobic environment—say, a compost pile or a municipal landfill—the greenhouse gas pollutes the atmosphere and the ammonia leaches into the soil and waterways. Folks are none too pleased.

However, when anaerobic decomposition occurs intentionally in giant structures called digesters, these and other by-products can be harnessed to create energy. Biogas, consisting of methane and carbon dioxide, can be altered to create electricity and heat or used as a natural gas replacement. Leftover liquids are recycled as a fertilizer. Digested solids find a new life as livestock bedding or landscaping products, including biodegradable pots.

Anaerobic digesters process food scraps, agricultural wastes such as manure, and biosolids (aka your poop). As more municipalities search for ways to reduce their environmental footprint and discover new uses for waste materials, an increasing number are turning to anaerobic digesters to divert organics and tap a renewable energy source. The next light switch you flip might be powered by apple cores.

Troubleshooting

So you've opened up your bokashi bucket and can immediately tell something is wrong. Maybe a rancid smell knocks you off your feet or your scraps are soaked—no, drowned—in liquid. Maybe nothing has happened at all and the french fries and General Tso's chicken look and smell entirely unchanged. How to right fermentation gone wrong?

Shig Matsukawa is a bokashi expert based in New York. A former student of Dr. Higa's, Shig has conducted research with the EM Research Organization (EMRO) in Japan and served as general manager for EMRO USA, which makes EM-1 in the United States. He now spreads education about the magic of microbes to countless urban composters like a generous dusting of bokashi flakes. Here are his tips for the weird, wonky, and whoa-my-gawd conditions that may occur in your bucket.

1. *Problem:* Food scraps don't smell like pickles, they smell like black death.

   Shig says: "You have to try to change the smell. There are many ways of doing it. Sometimes people put in really old food from the refrigerator that's already going south and pretty much rotting. When they put that in the bokashi bucket, add more bokashi flakes and sugars like fruit peels to feed [the microbes]. It will turn around. It doesn't kill all of the microbes that cause the rotting, but some of them will die and others will convert. Bacteria can interchange genetic material freely."

2. *Problem:* It's not just smelly in there, it's incredibly wet.

   Shig says: "The more liquidy it is, the more chance that the liquid part will oxidize more quickly than the solid part. Often it's the liquid that goes bad and makes it stinky. The solids are fine. Every now and then you can add some paper, napkins, brown paper bags, or stale bread to absorb liquid buildup.

   Microbes will feed off the cellulose. [If you have a drainage chamber], remove the liquid every two to three days.

3. *Problem:* Nothing's happening. No vinegar smell, no change in food scraps, and it's been weeks. Nada. Zip. Zilch.

  Shig says: "Near-odorless buckets are those that are almost dry. If your bucket is too dry, the fermentation will be slow. You will need to add more liquids—leftover juices, wine, salad dressing."

4. *Problem:* Last week's fried chicken has putrefied.

  Shig says: "With meats, you need to be a little more forceful managing it. They don't have the sugars or carbs needed to feed the microbes. If you have a healthy mix of fruits and vegetables, you can ferment the meat. And you don't just sprinkle it with bokashi [flakes], you cover it. Once, after Thanksgiving, there was a lot of turkey left over. I know that can go really bad. I did more than bokashi, I added activated EM: 'You're not going bad on me!'"

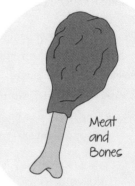

Meat and Bones

BURYING BOKASHI (FINALLY, FERMENTATION!)

Several weeks have passed since your last and final deposit. When you open up the bucket and peel back your bag layer, a vinegary tang fills the air. Perhaps white mold dusts your most recent feeding like a fine white snow—a common, but not mandatory, indication that things are going well. When you poke the scraps with your shovel or hand rake, you can tell structural integrity has broken down, making scraps surprisingly pliable, borderline mushy. Yay! Your scraps are good and fermented. It's time to transform the fermented food into soil.

  Bokashied scraps can be buried in any kind of soil, indoors or out. Use it to remediate dead, dry soils or to enhance the rich soil you've already got. You can bury scraps outdoors in yards, gardens, and raised beds or indoors in storage totes, buckets, and trash cans. They can also be added to a range of outdoor compost systems.

Outdoor Methods of Finishing Bokashi

Most people bury fermented scraps directly in soil, where the aerobic eco-system finishes their transformation into good, rich earth. After a few weeks, gardeners can plant directly on top of the soil where the bokashied scraps were buried. No need to turn, sift, or otherwise manage the food waste. You're good to go.

There are several ways to submerge your scraps.

TRENCHING

- Dig a hole or trench that is deep enough to hold your scraps plus an additional eight inches of soil on top.
- If there are plants nearby, make sure your hole is twelve inches away from any root systems. The high acidity of freshly fermented scraps can burn tender roots. (The acidity neutralizes with time.)
- Add the fermented food waste to the hole, mixing it with soil as it goes in to introduce aerobic microorganisms to the scraps. The more contact your fermented food scraps have with the soil universe, the easier it will be for them to break down.
- Cover the scraps with eight inches of soil.
- Walk away and have some fun.
- In a minimum of two weeks, you will be able to plant directly above your buried scraps. As a reminder, there is no need to turn, sift, or check soil temperature—nature will do the work for you. Depending on ambient conditions such as temperature and moisture levels, it may take longer.

Raised Beds

If you don't want to or can't bury your scraps underground, or if you have access only to a nonsoil (concrete, pavers, etc.) surface, you still have terrific options for burying your fermented food scraps outside. Build a raised bed at least a foot high and designate it as your bokashi burial ground. Alternate layers of soil and fermented scraps in the bed to create the most fertile growing medium around. Just be sure the depth of your bed will accommodate eight inches of soil on top of the final layer of scraps to prevent any local pests such as rodents from exploring. The likelihood is that pests will be repelled by the acidity of the scraps, but best practices help ensure that you (and your neighbors) have a positive experience with bokashi.

Aerobic Compost Piles

Got a bin, windrow, tumbler, or outdoor wormery? Add your bokashi scraps to it as you would any portion of greens, and maintain as usual. Note that worms may be sensitive to the acid levels present in newly fermented food waste, so add it slowly in small portions to one area of your bin. In time the pH neutralizes and the worms dig in; until then, don't worry if they steer clear of the material. They'll make their way there when it's ready. Remember to bury your bokashi in the pile, covering it with at least eight inches of bedding to avoid pests and to block odor.

BURIED TREASURE

In the 1970s a group of city gardeners bought a plot of land in Manhattan's East Village and transformed an area overrun by drugs, violence, and pests into an urban oasis. Decades later, El Sol Brillante community garden has become a verdant green center full of community activity in a hip, bustling neighborhood.

After experimenting with different composting methods, the gardeners at El Sol Brillante found that burying fermented food scraps worked wonders on their soil.

Now they not only host a public bokashi food-fermentation drop-off (and training)—where locals can bring scraps and sprinkle them with bokashi flakes—but have also rehabilitated the soil with bokashi at the Children's Garden up the block. They estimate they bury about eight thousand pounds of fermented food scraps a year.

Susan Greenfield, a lead volunteer bokashi-composter at El Sol Brillante and the Children's Garden, shares their story:

"This garden was started in the 1970s. Basically this area of the city was really run-down. People wouldn't go east of First Avenue.

"It was basically a war zone. People were dealing crack and cocaine, there was a shooting gallery here at [adjoining] Joseph C. Sauer Park. You could see prostitution. There was inactivity because of the rat epidemic on the block. You could literally see the ground moving, and it was really bad for many years.

"The value of the land was . . . forget about it. We were able to buy this plot for a crazy amount of money, like twenty-five hundred dollars, because nobody wanted to live here. They were able to buy this, we own it and it can't be taken away.

"[Early on,] there were cages on all of the plots; they had little locks. When I came in 1980, I tore down my fence and built benches. One by one, people decided they didn't want cages anymore.

"In 2009 we formed a compost committee. We had some bins that were retrofitted with hardware wire, and we bought an urban tumbler. [We were told] to put 50:50 carbon and nitrogen in the tumbler and let it sit for a week. When we opened it up, the methane was intense! Everybody cleared out of the garden. We were not popular, and the garden people were not happy with the compost.

"Around this time we met [the bokashi expert] Shig Matsukawa. [For Shig's bokashi troubleshooting tips, see page 124.] I read about EM and was like, this is scary. You pickle it and bury it? If we see one rat, the experiment is over and thank you very much. But it was working! The rats were really not going for the food. We put some in the urban tumbler with leaves and let it winter over. Come spring, there were millions of worms.

"We started with fifteen-dollar garbage pails, but they weren't airtight enough. Since this was really working, we decided to invest in bear-proof bins. We collect food waste from the community and show them how to mix it with bokashi. Only people with the garden key can come to El Sol Brillante to drop off, but we have a 24/7 drop-off at the Children's Garden, which is right down the street. We keep the gate ajar and have the bucket there and a team of people who come empty the bins and do the bokashi.

"At the drop-offs, we want to make it easy. There's a piece of paper on the bin with the starting date, and the date when it's full. In the cold weather, we wait one month after it's full. In warm weather, it's two weeks before fermentation works. Then it's ready to be converted into a soil mix.

"It can go into the tumblers or it can go into a huge, gigantic hole mixed with soil and leaves with at least a foot of soil on top. We are digging very deep with the trenches. Most of our trenching happens at the Children's Garden. The soil was dead. It was so white, so light and contaminated. You couldn't get a pitchfork into that soil. We have been trenching about four tons per year since 2009, and you figure one hundred bags of leaves per year, with a labor force of about three people. Now you can feel how soft the soil is.

"We grow kale and collards, string beans, tomatoes, and radishes. We can take the resources [from the community]. We literally have it all here to nourish the land and grow food."

Burying Bokashi Indoors

Replicate the great outdoors in your own indoor soil microcosm with a bucket, storage bin, or any other container.

Big planters are a great choice, because once you fill them with a soil-and-bokashi mix and let it sit a few weeks, you can plant directly in them. If you've got sad houseplants or even sadder housetrees that have been languishing in the same dead soil for years, consider transplanting them into pots with composted bokashi.

You can also designate one large container, such as a trash can or an eighteen-gallon storage bin, as your main soil maker. This will function like a raised bed as you layer soil and bokashi in it. If you choose to cover your large container between bokashi deposits, make sure there are holes for ventilation or that the lid is left slightly ajar.

Follow these steps to bury fermented food scraps indoors.

Step 1

Pour a few inches of soil into the bottom of your container. You can use purchased garden soil, soil from your potted plants, or even soil from outside. (Note: Bringing in outdoor soil means inviting in all the critters that might live in it, so don't panic if you see a roly-poly or two.)

Step 2

Add your fermented food scraps, mixing them with soil so the bokashi has contact with the soil microbes. When your scraps look fully dusted with soil, you're in good shape.

Step 3

Once you've added all of your food scraps, cover them up with about eight inches of soil. If you're using a pot that is shallower than that, then cover it with as much soil as you can, concentrating the bokashied scraps in the lower half of the plot. If you are using a lidded container, close it up. Make sure there are ventilation holes.

Step 4

Check in. Once a minimum of two weeks has passed, you can actually plant in the soil in your container. There may still be chunks of recognizable food waste in the lower layers of your container, but that's okay. They will break down over time (and will not rot, thanks to the fermentation). If your hope is to transform it all into soil before planting in it, use a garden fork or trowel to stir it up, circulating air, moisture, and microbes, and let it continue to compost.

A note on moisture: If the soil you're using is powdery and dry, add water to it. Since you have moved on to an aerobic phase of composting, you'll remember that water is essential to helping aerobic microbes get to work. Remember Armando the Wrung-Out Sponge when adjusting moisture levels.

 ### DIY: BOKASHI BUCKET WITH DRAINAGE

The easiest way to make a DIY bokashi bucket is to build a drainless system. All you need is an airtight bucket and . . . done. However, drainless systems might be a bit more challenging for beginners or people who crave precious bokashi juice for their drains, septic systems, or plants. This simple reservoir system takes only minutes to make.

YOU WILL NEED:

- 2 identical buckets that can be nested, creating a complete seal around the rim where they meet. If there is a gap, your fermentation process will fail.
- Drill with a ¼-inch drill bit
- Airtight lid

BUILDING AND USING YOUR BOKASHI BUCKET:

1. Drill 8–10 drainage holes in the bottom of one bucket.
2. Nest the bucket with the holes inside the bucket without holes.
3. Cover the upper bucket with an airtight lid.
4. Follow the care instructions on page 117.
5. To drain, pull the inner bucket away from the outer bucket. Pour the contents in the outer bucket down the drain or dilute it (see page 120 for the ratio) to feed soil and plants.
6. Rinse the inside of the outer bucket before renesting the inner bucket (optional).

DIY: INOCULATED BOKASHI FLAKES

You've gone bonkers for bokashi and find that you're flying through flakes more quickly than you anticipated. If the bokashi-flake bills are piling up, why not make your own for a fraction of the cost? Making your own also helps reduce your environmental footprint by reducing shipping and by recycling materials available locally, such as dried leaves or coffee chaff from a local roaster. The process is supereasy. It takes about fifteen minutes of work and a few weeks to ferment.

To make bokashi flakes, you will need to purchase a bottle of EM-1 serum. Since you use only a little at a time when making a batch, one bottle goes a long way. EM-1 is guaranteed to have the microbial group that is at the heart of the bokashi recipe, resulting in a more consistent result and potency each time. It's worth mentioning that some home bokashi brewers create their own serum, using rice water, milk, molasses, and time, cultivating something that is largely lacto-bacillus bacteria. While the resulting serum still inoculates flakes and ferments food, the results can vary.

The recipe below is adapted from TeraGanix, a company at the helm of sales and marketing of effective microorganisms in the United States.

TO MAKE FIVE POUNDS OF BOKASHI FLAKES, YOU WILL NEED:

- 2 tablespoons blackstrap, cane, or feed molasses to feed the microbes
- 5 cups water
- 2 tablespoons EM-1
- 5 pounds flake material (wheat bran, coffee chaff, crumpled dried leaves, or the like; the ideal material should be a dry brown that is easy to sprinkle and won't clump up)

- Pot or bucket big enough to mix all of the above
- Plastic bag large enough to store the bran while it ferments
- Tarp or other surface large enough for you to dry the fermented flakes on

MAKING THE FLAKES:

1. Dissolve the molasses in the water.
2. Add the EM-1 to the water.
3. Put the flake material in the pot or bucket and mix the liquid into it little by little. Periodically, squeeze a handful of flakes into a ball. If it holds its shape and no extra liquid comes out, you've achieved the desired moisture content. If it is too dry, continue to add more liquid until you achieve the proper levels. If it's too wet, you will need more flake material.
4. When the flakes are ready, put them in the plastic bag. Squeeze all the air out of the bag and tie it up tight.
5. Store the bag someplace warm for a minimum of two weeks. You can let it sit for longer, as your schedule requires.
6. Check in on your flakes. After several weeks, they should have a mild vinegar smell and may have white mold on them if they fermented properly. If you have black or green mold, something went wrong. Air may have gotten into your product or it may have been too wet. Discard it in a compost pile or throw it away and start over.
7. Use the finished bokashi wet for up to two weeks. Keep it stored in an airtight container. To dry your flakes for long-term use and storage, lay your flakes out in a thin layer on a tarp, flat plastic bag, or other surface. Bright hot sun on a windless day works great, but your living room floor is fine too. The amount of time it takes for flakes to dry depends on a few environmental factors. The warmer and dryer it is, and the thinner you spread your flakes out, the faster they will dry.
8. Once the flakes are dry, store them in an airtight bag or container in a cool place. Your finished bokashi flakes should last for several years.

8 URBAN FARMYARD

Farm folks reap great benefit from livestock, harvesting cow pies, horse apples, sheep dung, and goat pellets to fertilize their soil. While you may not have a little house on the prairie, there are plenty of cute, cuddly pets from your studio apartment or townhouse that can happily enhance your compost pile with their own homemade "gifts." In addition to being packed with nutrients and nitrogen, manure is full of organic matter that helps improve soil content and structure. It's a wonderful green item for your compost pile and, as pet owners can attest, a seemingly endless renewable resource.

Manures—and yes, your pet's droppings officially become manure once they're deployed as fertilizer—are as different as the animals that make them. Factors such as diet, digestive microbe populations, and the general health of an animal all influence the quality of an animal's poop and how it is best managed when composted. Since dung comes in all shapes, sizes, textures, and smells, you may have limitations on how much you can practically and safely process in your small-space system. Though city and suburban composters have hearts and ambition as big as their countryside counterparts, they certainly don't have the same acreage. Figuring out how to best incorporate manures into your compost pile takes a few careful calculations.

Most animals in urban and suburban jungles are more guinea pig than actual swine, but the changing landscape of urban livestock and increased engagement with local farms means the barnyard is creeping into backyards across the country. Chickens and goats have become welcome neighbors in many municipalities, and plenty of towns border cow and goat pastures. Plus, you know those horse-and-buggy rides so popular in your town square or park, and those police officers astride trusty steeds? Those horses live and eat somewhere nearby . . . which means their poop is closer than you think.

If you're looking to bolster your compost with manure but don't have any critters to call your own, consider connecting with local animal owners such as that cute neighbor with the chicken coop. And as you'll read later, you're welcome to stray from traditional manures and embrace your Labradoodle's doo-doos.

The droppings of your furry and feathered babies may seem insignificant when you sweep them up. Collectively, they add up to billions of pounds of poop each year in the United States alone. Why not harvest Thumper's and Spot's droppings and use them to feed your garden instead of sending them off to the landfill?

Read on to learn how.

SAFETY FIRST

Composting pet poop is a bit more complicated than tossing an orange peel into a pile of leaves. Droppings consist of organic matter that has taken a long journey down a digestive tract, and it's possible it has picked up some nasty passengers along the way. Some poops have the potential to carry harmful pathogens such as salmonella, E. coli, or cryptosporidium, all of which can make humans sick. They may also contain unsavory creatures like parasitic roundworms that can make their way into humans and make them ill.

Thermophilic composting is the best way to destroy poop pathogens. When compost hits over 131 degrees Fahrenheit for a minimum of three consecutive days, pathogens get thoroughly fried. Another benefit to hot composting is the destruction of undigested weed seeds that may have made their way into poop from an animal's feed. However, as you read in chapter 4, thermophilic composting isn't always a practical option for casual composters with limited space or little inclination to manage a pile so large.

Aging manure before composting it also helps reduce the pathogen load, as pathogens die off after time. The Washington State University Extension office recommends aging manure for at least one year before using it in compost piles. If you're in no rush to use it and have a place to store it, wait even longer.

The most common manures for composting come from herbivores such as cows and small omnivores with mostly vegetarian diets such as chickens. While it's possible to compost the droppings of animals with meat-heavy diets, these manures require delicate handling because of odor and pathogens. Once composted, carnivore or meat-heavy omnivore manures are best used on ornamental (vs. edible) plants and in areas that are not heavily trafficked. Don't frolic in a field of dreams that's really a field of nightmares.

Now, this isn't to worry you. Millions of happy, healthy pet owners safely deal with pet droppings each and every day, whether they compost them or collect them to toss in the trash. Simply consider this a friendly public service announcement to encourage safe manure-composting practices.

GET THE SCOOP ON POOP

Whether you plan to source manures from others (who knew your niece's bunny was cute *and* useful?) or compost your own little darling's droppings, know the answers to the following questions before you begin:

- Is the animal fed low-grade food made with processed fillers, chemicals, or other impurities you may not want in your compost? These include plant-based feed such as hay treated with persistent pesticides and other chemicals that may compromise the quality or safety of your compost.
- Is the animal on any medication, such as dewormer, that may affect your compost ecosystem? As the name of the medication suggests, an active dewormer could kill off the lovely earthworms hard at work in your pile.
- What conditions does the animal live in? Think free-roaming chicken in a sprawling, grassy backyard versus caged chicken in a cramped poultry barn standing in weeks of its own poop. The better the conditions the animal lives in, the better the chances the animal is robust and healthy and not exposed to anything harmful.
- How well has the health of the animal been maintained? Regular doctor checkups, diet, exercise, and so on all factor into the strength of the animal and its immune system.

Since the items you feed your pile will eventually feed your soil (and in the case of edible gardens, go on to feed you), it's important to provide the best-quality ingredients you can.

CREATURE COMFORTS

Tucked on an island off the southern tip of Manhattan, reachable only by boat, resides a menagerie of goats, chickens, bunnies, and worms. They eat, poop, and graze the land to teach New Yorkers all about composting.

Earth Matter's Compost Learning Center on Governors Island, a public park in New York Harbor, introduces core compost concepts to visitors. Earth Matter is a host of the NYC Compost Project and regularly processes thousands of pounds of food scraps as part of the NYC Department of Sanitation's Local Organics Recovery Program. They also compost landscaping and vendor food waste from Governor Island events.

Here is Marisa DeDominicis, who cofounded Earth Matter with Kendall Morrison and Charlie Bayrer in 2009, on caring for their compost zoo:

"One reason we came to Governors Island was we felt the people there were open to the experience of composting. It wasn't like we tried to do it on Forty-Second Street, stopping people during their busy days. People come to the Island because of their families, their sweethearts, to check out an event or to ride bikes. They find us and just keep coming back.

"During the second year of our Compost Learning Center, we got twenty chicks. We really wanted the chickens because we saw it as a way to show how they were part of the cycle.

"We found that from an early age the chickens really like a lot of food scraps. We put the scraps out in the morning and scrape them up at the end of the day before it gets dark. Chickens generally eat throughout the day. They like fresh greens more than the cooked kale [that some people drop off]. Think about them foraging—they're eating fresh stuff, not cooked stuff. In the summer, they live exclusively on food scraps. If they need grain, they get it from the bread. If they need corn, there are a lot of vendors [on Governors Island] who sell corn on the cob. So they get a lot of the nutrients they need. [After we move the scraps to the] compost pile, the chickens help peck and scratch at the bugs on the pile. They know where to go.

"We liked that chicken manure was really rich in nitrogen and really good for composting. Chickens are creatures of habit and will poop in the same area, so we are doing deep-layer bedding. We put [down] a good layer of straw shavings [where they like to poop] over and over again. It's always a fresh layer of bedding, so they are not stepping on their poop. Then over two years we will not turn it. We will not do anything. We will leave it.

"In our third year we said, let's add goats. They're cute! There is a farm in Long Island that has goats, and we foster two of them from May until October; then they return back in the fall. That's two less mouths for the farmer to feed during the time of milk and honey, before the goats have to go to work getting pregnant and producing milk for their babies and to make cheese for the farmer. They also became more docile because of all of the attention the public gives them, which the farmer wants.

"The goats really like landscaping greens such as trees. So the best thing about

Governors Island isn't necessarily all of the food scraps, it's all of the yard waste they generate. We knew we would get more buy-in from the landscapers for our compost endeavor because of the goats. The goats were a way to make the landscapers' *aha* moment go off.

"Both the goats and the chickens are pasturers, and the idea is to have them help where the soil has become compacted because the land is overused. The parkland is dusty. You want it to be loamy and healthy; you don't want it to be overpacked. We don't really want to pick up the goat [poop], we want it to be fertilizing.

"Our bunnies like carrot tops, fresh shoots. They say the bunny poop is the best food for worms, so I have a worm bin that catches the poop when [the bunnies] are in their hutches at night. It has a wire mesh bottom on one half. The whole idea is that the worms go crazy over the rabbit poop because the bunnies are vegetarians. Rabbits are particularly wonderful for the nitrogen content.

"The animals are something. Volunteers come because there are these amazing creatures out here and people want the connection to them. We are always learning from the animals—we are learning a lot."

For more information, please visit https://earthmatter.org.

Manure Menagerie

Wondering if your pet's poop is a compost contender? Here's a peek at common household-animal and urban-livestock manures.

Freshwater Aquarium Fish

Watching fish may lower your blood pressure, but using their wastewater to improve soil health can lower your carbon footprint.

When you clean your fish-tank filter and all the grimy gravel below, the mucky water siphoned out is full of fish poop. While most people chuck it, fish-poop water is actually a key source of nutrients in aquaponic farming, a cycle in which fish excrement feeds plants that, by eating it, purifies the water for the fish. That aquaponic pepper you recently purchased at the farmers market? Uh-huh—packed with fish pootrients.

Using tank water on your plants and in your compost system is simple. Pour your dirty tank water onto a dry compost pile or feed it directly to plants. If the water has an exceptionally high amount of waste (that is, nitrogen) in it, consider diluting it before direct feeding.

Two quick notes:

1. If you add a chemical supplement to treat your water, check the ingredients to make sure your plants can tolerate them.
2. Saltwater aquarium water should not be added to plants and soil, as the high salt content can harm plants.

Reptiles and Amphibians

Reptile and amphibian owners know that most of their scaly or slimy friends naturally carry the salmonella bacterium in their intestines. The risk is the trade-off we make for the pleasure of gazing into their weird, prehistoric grins.

While it's not recommended that small children, pregnant women, the elderly, or folks with weak immune systems own reptiles, healthy people with robust immune systems should be fine if they handle Kermit, Fang, and all their droppings with care.

Because of the risk of exposure to salmonella, use these droppings only in a hot compost pile or to fertilize soil for nonedibles in areas with little foot traffic.

Birds: Cage and Coop Poop

Birds of a feather all poop together, and their droppings—plus the carbon-rich newspaper or straw they've landed in—can all go in the compost pile. If you've got a parakeet, pair of lovebirds, or flock of backyard chickens, you're sitting on a black goldmine of nitrogen-rich greens.

- Caged birds that twitter from indoor perches usually relieve themselves on bedding at the bottom of their cages. If you use an approved brown such as shredded newspaper, you can dump the entire thing into your pile. Some pet birds can transmit chlamydiosis in their droppings, which causes flu-like symptoms (and is not to be confused with the human version of chlamydia, which is contracted an entirely different way). Their droppings may also carry salmonella, avian tuberculosis, and giardia.

- Many city dwellers are clucking about urban chickens. As any chicken keeper knows, the birds are as prolific poopers as they are egg layers; the average hen makes about forty-five pounds of poop each year. Extremely high in nitrogen, and rich in phosphorous and potassium to boot, chicken poop is used worldwide to feed soil and plants. Depending on how you keep your coop, you can collect poop and bedding daily for composting, or you can pile layers of fresh bedding on top of soiled bedding. As time passes, older layers break down and can be added to your pile at your convenience.

Small Furry Animals

Rabbits, hamsters, guinea pigs, and gerbils are cute little pellet poopers that make magnificent soil food for your compost pile.

The most popular of this crew for composters? Bunnies! Their droppings are super-high in nitrogen with a carbon-to-nitrogen ratio of 4:1, making them a great green for your pile. Put a catch tray underneath the wire mesh bottom of a typical rabbit hutch to collect bunny poop. Empty the tray (with bedding material) into your compost pile as needed. Or if you are a vermicomposter, install your worm bin directly under your bunnies. Worms will delight in rainstorms of bunny poop. If pee and worm-bin-appropriate bedding fall in, no problem. That will break down too. Just make sure to keep your greens and browns balanced, as the high nitrogen content of rabbit poop and pee may require supplemental browns.

Traditional Livestock: Horses, Goats, Cows, Sheep

When you were little you always wanted a pony. Now that you're all grown up, all you want is pony poop. Oh, how times have changed.

You may not have a horse, cow, or other classic farm beast, but that doesn't mean they aren't all over your town or city. Is there a park or waterfront that boasts horse-drawn buggy rides? Is there a stable, farm, or petting zoo nearby? If you put your mind to it, there's a good chance you may be able to score some farmyard poop.

Now, practically speaking, our hooved homies tend to be quite large. As you can imagine, their poop matches in stature. Your system must be big enough to accommodate the manure you collect. If the manure is sourced from elsewhere, remember you'll also need a practical and community-friendly way to transport it. If the manure is fresh, you will also need space to age it. Compost these manures exclusively outdoors—your roommates are welcome to send me thank-you cookies for insisting.

Cats

So far, composting pet poops has been straightforward and easy peasy. Leave it to cunning cats to cause mischief and discord—composting cat poop is a total no-no.

Really, just don't.

Cat poops are truly toxic—never, ever compost them.

Feline feces can be home to a parasitic protozoan that causes toxoplasmosis in humans, an illness resulting in brain damage, disease, and defects. Eggs of this malicious microbe can live in soil for up to a year. People with weak immune systems and pregnant women (and their babies)

Compost-Friendly Pet Poop

Glub Glub!

Fish poop!

Here, fishy, fishy!

Chicken poop!

Chicken poop is a potent green.

Go ahead and compost snake poop!

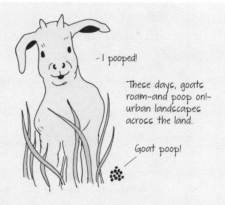

- I pooped!

These days, goats roam—and poop on!—urban landscapes across the land.

Goat poop!

Yup, you can compost their poop.

Turtle poop!

are at particular risk. It's generally recommended to dispose of cat waste and cat litter in the trash in sealed plastic bags.

Dogs

Fido? More like Fi-doo.

Doggy doo can be home to a range of worms, parasites, and not-so-nice bacteria. Because dogs are omnivores, their waste also tends to stink. What to do with their poo?

Dog poop is actually commonly composted, and several commercial composting products exclusively target dog waste. Many of them are digester-like systems that operate a lot like a canine septic system. Just remember to always compost your dog poop separately from your food scraps.

If you collect your dog poop in compostable bags, please note that these bags are largely designed to decompose in industrial composting facilities and not in a backyard composting system (for more on compostable products, see page 175).

ZOO DOO

Looking for the latest on the upcoming Fecal Fest or Holidoo giveaway? Then dial 206-625-POOP for a hilarious and informative message peppered with more poop puns than you can count.

Seattle's Woodland Park Zoo was the first in the country to compost their collection of exotic droppings in their Zoo Doo compost product. Humor has been a big part in wooing the public into loving the poo. Since its inception in the mid-1980s, the zoo's composted giraffe, oryx, hippo, gazelle, zebra, and elephant dung has become so poopular that only winners in a special lottery are lucky enough to nab a bag.

Here's Zoo Doo program founder Jeff Gage on the early days of the 'Doo:

"The most amazing thing about Zoo Doo is it was the first composted zoo doo in the country. Portland canned their manure fresh in tin cans, until some exploded!

"The zoo had a head gardener who was stockpiling [manure] and using what she wanted for the grounds. She asked the Seattle engineering department for some help setting up [manure composting] as a regular program. I was bugging the engineering department to start neighborhood composting systems, and they asked if I was interested in shoveling manure at the zoo. I, of course, said yes.

"I guided the zoo through several steps to develop an operation plan and get approvals from the health department. We kept all the carnivores out of the collected manures and only [composted] herbivore and aviary waste. This included just who you might imagine: elephants, which eat mostly hay; hippos, which eat aquatic materials, grass, and pumpkins. It was done in windrows that are about forty feet long by twelve feet wide and seven feet deep. They are turned once a week and rewatered after the first two turns.

"I did a pathogen study for three months and then got the zoo's marketing plan together.

"Our slogan was 'For all you doo, this doo's for you.'

"We had a tough time convincing the engineering department to go along with the 206-625-POOP gimmick, but they did and it worked. It got us on Jeopardy and The Tonight Show. Humor sells! We had such a big response the first day of sales that we had to go to an appointment system to handle the traffic. Then a few years later, we had to go on a lottery system, as so many people wanted to get some.

"It was 1985. The contract and full system cost for operations was $30,000 the first year, and we brought in $60,000 in income from sales! The zoo adopted the program directly the following year.

"Compost is not gross—it's the essence of purity, the conversion of poo to plant. With properly composted poo, everyone smiles and takes a deep, appreciative whiff."

For more information, please visit: www.zoo.org/conservation/zoodoo.

Handling Manure

Now that you have a handle on which poops you can compost, it's time to get a handle on handling the poop itself.

Below is a list of best practices for dealing with animal manures. If you're a pet owner, you may already be familiar with this list of tips.

If handling animal poop is as new to you as your neighbor's chicken coop (they offered you free eggs in exchange for cleaning out droppings . . . why not add it to your compost pile?), rest assured these steps are easy to execute with little fuss.

- Thoroughly wash your hands with soap and water for at least twenty seconds after handling the animal and/or its poop.
- Clean the surfaces the animal and its poop come into contact with, including its cage or tank if it lives with you. (A veterinarian can recommend an appropriate cleaner to use.)
- Do not place animal habitats or waste-disposal containers such as litter boxes near human food or food preparation areas.
- Wear protective gloves when handling manures to help stay germ-free.

HOW TO COMPOST ANIMAL MANURE

What to do with all the poo? The following are common methods used to process animal wastes.

Hot Composting (Great for All Compostable Pet Waste)

As mentioned above, thermophilic composting is the best way to process poop because the heat destroys pathogens. If your pile reaches 131 degrees Fahrenheit for a minimum of three days, the pathogens inside will pass on to the great compost bin in the sky.

If you don't have a thermophilic pile, the small NatureMill machine (page 55) can handle pet waste in its thermophilic chamber. However, this may be a very stinky method if you choose to use it indoors.

Remember, never compost cat waste!

Digesters (Perfect for Dogs)

Send animal wastes to the bowels of your yard by burying them in a digester. Pet-waste digesters are a popular means of disposing of animal waste for prolific poopers such as dogs. Many people with yards simply make their own digesters (page 75) and toss in their dog's piles daily. Time, microbes, worms, and other critters do all the hard work of transforming it into compost.

Bury your digester in soil with good drainage, far away from edible plants. Place it as far away from any water bodies as possible: you don't want any pathogens leaching into your lovely fish pond. Try not to submerge the digester on a hill, as anything growing downhill of it may take up pathogens through the soil or from water traveling through the soil.

As you can imagine, an inground container packed with droppings has the potential to get a bit stinky. If your nose objects to the smell when you open your digester, toss in a layer of browns to cover the topmost poop layer.

Several commercial systems are specifically marketed as pet-waste digesters. They offer additional additives like septic starter or features specifically tailored toward processing waste, such as poop-digesting bacteria and enzymes. Bokashi juice (page 122), bokashi flakes (page 132), and activated EM-1 may also help reduce odor and speed along decomposition.

Vermicomposting (Great for Small-Animal Droppings)

Red wigglers love, love, love a good pile of manure, and they're not particular about the type they get. Whether they're rolling in rabbit poop, cavorting in cow pies, or even digging through doggy doo, they're happy to munch the day away.

Enclosing a large volume of animal waste in an indoor worm bin is just asking for a roommate revolt—and a revolting scenario. If you have large loads of manure, place your worm bin outside or consider another method of composting. If you've got a bunny or other small herbivore with a manageable poop load, add the animal's poop to your indoor worm bin or flow-through system just as if it were a regular green. Better yet, if the animal poops in an appropriate worm-bin bedding (page 140), then you can add the bedding to the bin as a brown.

Two notes of caution:

- Don't vermicompost manure from an animal taking dewormers. Even though medicine potency fades with time, you don't want the dewormer to deworm your worm pile with poison.
- Animal waste can be very high in nitrogen, and may heat up if added in excess or in a dense clump. As with any feedstock in a wormery, begin by adding tiny amounts of manure to your bin to see how your worms and the environment respond to it (see page 83). Adjust your portions as best suits the worms.

Outdoor Nonthermophilic Aerobic Compost Piles
(Great for All Animals with Compostable Manure Except Dogs)

Manure can be processed in active or passive compost piles. Back on the farm, plenty of folks pile their animal poop in a corner, mix bedding materials with it, and let it sit for several months to a year. If they've got time in their long workday, or if making compost quickly is a priority, they check in and give a turn. Over time, it turns into black gold. Replicate this process in your own backyard heap.

Fermentation and Burial (Great for All Compostable Pet Wastes)

Fans of bokashi use anaerobic microbes to pickle poop for burial. As discussed in chapter 7, the microbes in EM-1 are used for various agricultural-waste and septic-system treatments. The process is easily adapted for pet-waste systems. You'll recall that the high acidity created by fermentation kills off pathogens and transforms odor with its vinegary scent. Right there, two major concerns of pet-waste composting are taken care of.

Purchase a commercial bokashi pet-waste system or make your own (page 131).

A Note on Humanure

Uh-huh. That word means exactly what it sounds like. Around the world, and throughout history, people have used human manure to help enrich soil.

These days, many humanure practitioners bring their outhouse logic indoors with a range of innovative systems to keep their waste out of the septic systems and in the life cycle of the soil. From simple DIY buckets with toilet lids attached (a perfect place for that zebra-print seat you've always wanted to use) to complex manufactured systems that aerate, heat, and turn your contributions, there's something at every price point, for every walk of life. And compost toilet systems aren't just for hippies. The Bronx Zoo in New York City is just one of many major landmarks to have composting toilets as part of its greener landscapes.

The bible of this movement is *The Humanure Handbook* by Joseph Jenkins. The book makes a passionate argument for conserving water (so many flushes) and tapping a readily available resource that you make all by yourself, each and every day. It also offers instructions on how to build your own systems and work them into your compost piles, whether you're looking for an alternative to a Porta-Potty at an event you're planning, trying to live off the grid, or wanting to bring a sleek eco-innovation into your home.

9 GET ORGANIZED! COMMUNITY COMPOSTING

Sometimes it takes a village to raise a compost pile.

I bet my banana peels that there are people on your block, in your apartment building, or at your dog run who have the same interest in composting that you do. If you cast your net even further, to schools, community and garden groups, places of worship, and your workplace, you may find an entire army that can elevate your compost plans to unprecedented heights.

Whether you have joint custody of a worm bin with your neighbor or you're processing literally tons of food waste with a school, community composting is a great way to share the responsibility and effort of a pile.

Composting on a group level offers plenty of benefits:

- Shared organizational and maintenance responsibilities. Your life is hectic enough. Having extra sets of hands means your vision need not be compromised because you're overextended.
- More material can be processed than you could do alone. Say you aren't satisfied with simply composting your morning coffee grounds. You want to make a difference on a grand scale. More people means more able bodies

and minds to help you tackle food waste from a local juice bar or a work-place cafeteria.

- A bigger project is more inclusive, allowing different types of people to par-ticipate. Not everyone with green inklings has the inclination to turn a pile. But that doesn't mean they can't contribute. As your project grows, your net-work of people with valuable resources to offer such as space, web devel-opment, and fundraising does too. (More on working with volunteers later in this chapter.)

- Launch social change. Hopefully, the stories from the real-life community composters in this book have demonstrated the potential of grassroots efforts. When communities are galvanized for a cause, their potential for success and motivating a movement are huge.

- Cut costs for your group or garden project. If your community pays hand over fist for waste hauling, soil-related garden supplies, or water for land-scaping, composting can help ease the burden. By diverting food waste and creating rich soil that holds nutrients and water, you reduce costs.

- It's fun. This point cannot be overstated. It's wonderful (and good for you) to unplug yourself every now and again and get out into nature with family, colleagues, or complete strangers who may soon become friends. Nothing bonds a group more than groping worms or turning pitchforks full of food scraps. I've been lucky to find there are very few diva composters. These folks get dirty and cozy up with critters of all kinds and dare to dream they can help bring about change one rind at a time. Plus—look in the mirror, budding composter. They're a good-looking bunch.

JOIN A MOVEMENT

It's amazing what can happen when a few people start composting . . . and tell a few other people who start composting with them . . . who then tell a whole bunch more. . . .

There's a good chance that there's a lot more compost cooking in your area than you realize, and these projects might need an extra set of hands. Why not meet peers and dive deep into a hands-on education with a compost project already in the works?

A quick Web search of local organizations or community-building hubs such as meetup.com can connect you with composting projects in your area. Or, familiarize yourself with green groups who may have piles in need of TLC.

Who's a good bet?

- Master Composter and Master Gardener programs
- Community gardens
- Eco-minded shops or eateries
- Farmers markets
- Garden clubs
- Schools
- Recycling initiatives
- Local farms (and that includes urban ones)

If you can't find a project that suits your goals or interests, or if you have an idea that's making your toes tingle with glee, then don't hesitate. Be the catalyst of your very own community composting project. Sound daunting? Take a sip of lemonade and relax, it doesn't have to be.

START A MOVEMENT

It all begins with a plan. Start with a basic concept you know has a high likelihood of succeeding. It's always better to be a smashing success on a small scale than to shoot for the moon and end up sputtering at takeoff. Launching a citywide compost program for all school cafeterias may be overly ambitious right out of the gate, but starting in your child's elementary school with the help of your PTA can lead to widespread change (see page 164 for a true story).

Once you've wowed the world with the winning Phase One of your project—proving to skeptics that making compost doesn't have to be smelly, costly, or pest infested to succeed—develop and pitch a fabulous Phase Two. By this time you'll be armed with plenty of experience and insight regarding how your project works and have a strong inkling of how to improve it.

Take a breath, go slow, and have your notebook and pen at the ready. Here is the first set of questions to ask yourself when developing your plan:

Where Are You Going to Compost?

The limited space in bustling cities and towns can make landing real estate for composting a challenge. The space available to you for composting will dictate what kind of pile you create and how it is managed. Location also determines what communities your pile may intersect with and whether there are permissions that must be granted or ordinances to follow before you make your dream come true. Possible spots for a community compost pile include the following:

- Your yard
- A friend or neighbor's yard, or the yard belonging to your condo, co-op, or rented apartment building
- Your workplace
- A community garden or urban farm
- A classroom or school
- Churches, synagogues, temples, and other places of worship
- Municipal spaces such as libraries or parks
- Abandoned or neglected lots
- Restaurants, cafés, juice bars, coffee shops

HOW DOES YOUR GARDEN GROW?

Originally founded as a project of the Mid-South Peace and Justice Center, Grow-Memphis is a core Tennessee institution bringing food justice to low-income and struggling communities. Now an independent nonprofit, GrowMemphis works to establish fair food policy and helps train individuals in the creation of community gardens. A big part of their garden initiatives is compost and compost education. Here is Chris Peterson, GrowMemphis's executive director (2012–2014), on how composting fits into the community-garden model:

"Even though we are in the Delta, we have really awful soil, really hard, dense clay. You can't grow much, and you can't seem to buy good soil around here. We end up doing a lot of raised-bed gardening because there is a lot of contamination in the soil locally—a lot of lead and a lot of stones, concrete, or bricks.

"Composting is really important to us because it is free. We work with primarily low-income communities that don't have a lot of resources. We are a small organization and we have limited resources ourselves. If you don't have any money, buying soil is kind of out of the question. So you end up needing to make it.

"[As far as securing garden and composting space], there is no one way to do it. Our county government will take control of delinquent properties on a regular basis and have all of those mapped up for tax sale as part of our Shelby County Land Bank, a repository of information on vacant lots. They will give property to nonprofit organizations for free just to get them off the cash rolls.

"Most of our gardens will be owned by a church or other nonprofit in the neighborhood. We have had luck with a person who just has a vacant lot who is sick of paying somebody to come and mow it twice a month. The person will say, 'I'm happy to let you guys use it in perpetuity if you promise I don't have to pay to mow it anymore.'

"We help our gardeners with lease agreements, and the biggest thing is to put everything in writing. I can't advise that strongly enough. Handshake agreements are the ones that end up going poorly. You think the other person has a clear understanding of what you are trying to do, and for whatever reason the other party isn't happy. Even if it's handwritten, get something in writing. Also, have some sort of clause to reevaluate the relationship. If it's not every season, at least every two or three years, sit down together and reevaluate where you are. Just be as clear with expectations as possible. If you're worried about the way people are composting in your lot, have all of those situations hammered out.

"Composting is a really powerful symbol of the work that we do: When you are composting you are literally taking waste and turning it into a primary source of soil fertility. We are taking vacant lots that are essentially considered waste and transforming them into really powerful places, not just of food production but of community building. And some of the people we work with are largely people the rest of society has given up on, chronically unemployed or from low-income communities. They become the backbone of the work. We are talking about building a new local food system that is based around people and rebuilding communities and community relations."

For more information, visit: http://growmemphis.org.

What Kind of System Will You Be Using?

Determine what, if any, limitations or constraints there are on the system of your dreams. Laws and regulations vary from town to town, state to state, building to building, backyard to backyard. Here's a list of possible laws and ordinances for you to look into before you begin:

- Small-scale and backyard composting rules designated by your town: Reach out to your local government and see if there are any backyard composting rules regarding, for example, unacceptable compost materials or location restrictions.
- Homeowners rules: Check in with your condo or co-op board, landlord, or homeowners association for any guidelines a compost project must follow (or to see if it is even allowed). There's a good chance these folks may lean toward an instant no, as they don't want to add compost to their already

substantial pile of concerns in running a location. For tips on how to pitch your project, check out the suggestions on page 163.

- Business and residential waste-disposal and recycling ordinances: Usually enforced by your local department of sanitation (though sometimes a sustainability office will have answers), these laws focus on the legalities of what constitutes trash, how it is to be disposed of, and who can collect or use it.

- Financial status for individuals or organizations (if you plan to receive donations or earn money through the sale of services or products): General information about establishing nonprofit status and the like is readily available on the Internet. However, it may help to speak with an accountant about the nuances of your plan.

- Regulations on food-waste and pest management: Often overseen by the health department in your area, these rules may provide guidelines on how to safely manage local pests and organic waste.

IF YOU BUILD IT, THEY WILL COME

In the beginning, New York City's Lower East Side Ecology Center (LESEC) just wanted to collect compostables to make soil for their East Village garden. Already stewards of recycling, they invited neighbors to bring by their peels and coffee grounds. The program took off, and LESEC soon brought their drop-off program to Manhattan's bustling Union Square Greenmarket.

Launching a food-scrap drop-off model has exploded into a citywide phenomenon. The Greenmarket drop-off program, now run by GrowNYC, invites local residents to bring food scraps to collection bins when they come to shop at dozens of greenmarkets citywide. By crowdsourcing food waste, greenmarkets collected more than *two million* pounds of food scraps in its first two years.

The LESEC hosts a range of recycling, composting, and ecological education classes and is one of the hosts of NYC's Master Composter certification. They also sell compost and potting soil made from NYC's leftover fruits and veggies.

Here's LESEC cofounder Christine Datz-Romero on their amazing story:

"In 1990 we got a lease from the city of New York for some empty lots on the Lower East Side. At that point we had been doing community-based recycling for three years. We had this space and wanted to make it look pretty. Since we had no budget to buy soil, we said, 'Let's make our own.'

"We asked the people who brought us their metal and plastic to bring us their food scraps to compost. Then, later on, we approached the Union Square Greenmarket to see if we could start a collection program there. We thought it was a good constituency because people who go to the market on a regular basis are cooks, they have a lot of food scraps, and they are plugged in to the whole idea of sustainability. The Greenmarket was very open to the idea.

"We started out with a table and waited for people to come by and ask what we were doing. Once we started collecting food scraps, we also brought a worm bin to show people how they could compost at home. We wanted to raise awareness about composting and empower people either to start their own bin or to participate in our program.

"We moved to East River Park in 1998 and raised money to create an in-vessel composting system. We got a license and went to pick up food scraps from selected businesses, because at that point, there were no commercial carters. The other thing we did was produce a product, screening the compost and bringing it back to the market to sell to defray some of the operating costs we incurred running the program.

"You really have to plug in to your constituency and make sure they support you, not only by bringing new materials and letting their friends know, but by making monetary contributions. Earned income through the sale of your products is also a good thing, because it gives you independence.

"It really takes an effort to sustain a program because participation is built slowly. You just need to be diligent about getting the word out, being there, and being consistent. To have a successful program, you need to communicate to the public that it's really important. [If it's challenging,] you can't just cut it and decide later you want to start it again, because the credibility of the program really suffers."

For more information, please visit http://lesecologycenter.org and www.grownyc.org.

Who Do You Need Permission or Approvals From?

Ah, the people factor, which at times can be trickier to handle than a whopping pile of rotting trash. People can be very protective about the spaces they visit and inhabit. To get this project off the ground, educate and arm yourself before you make the pitch. You'll likely have to work with and convince a range of people with very different concerns, so knowing your audiences can go a long way. Ask yourself the following questions:

1. Who is in charge of this space? "In charge of" can mean a lot of things. Owners, managers, boards, and groundskeepers are just some of the folks who have a say in the different care and management aspects of a space. Knowing who people are, what they do, and what their concerns might be will have you prepared to address them. For example, while a maintenance chief may run the waste management of a school, it may be the custodial and cafeteria staffs who have direct daily contact with the food waste. Each group will have their own set of questions for you, pertaining to their daily tasks and responsibilities.

2. Who uses this space? Gardeners in a community garden, children in a classroom, runners in a local park . . . you get the drift. It's possible these people may need a bit of convincing as well, so put yourselves in their shoes and brainstorm what their concerns might be.

3. Are there any limitations to scale, size, number of people, and the like who can use or access this space at a given time, in given hours? It's important to understand the practical governance of your compost project's new home. Will helpers need a key to access the space? Is it available to you and your group only during certain hours? Can the space accommodate only a handful of people at a time, forcing your to organize your compost cadre in shifts?

Who Will Join You in This Endeavor?

Sure, knowing that Jimmy and Joanie are super into composting is nice, but when push comes to shoveling, what amount of time, energy, or support are Jimmy, Joanie, and the rest of the crew really going to put in?

Work within everyone's realistic means and capabilities and avoid an idealized dream version full of the best of intentions but the worst of execution.

Volunteers

Most grassroots projects rely heavily on the generosity of volunteers with free Saturday afternoons, a pair of work gloves, and an unstoppable zeal to make things happen.

Here are some easy ways enthusiastic volunteers can participate directly in the care and maintenance of your compost project:

- Hosting a bin or pile in their space
- Volunteering time or skills to build, feed, turn, or harvest a compost pile
- Donating or collecting compostable materials and gardening supplies

Not everyone is a turner, wormer, or food-waste slinger. The skills and passions needed to grow a community compost project and allow it to flourish are as vast and varied as the soil ecosystem is. Don't worry if some of your most ardent supporters refuse to get within shovel's reach of a worm. There are plenty of ways they can pitch in without getting their hands dirty.

Here are some key ways to incorporate a wide range of participants (and a few tasks you might not have realized could be on your to-do list):

- Canvassing: Someone's gotta pound the pavement—both online or in real life. Whether they're getting signatures, scoring tools, or pitching business or community partners to support your effort, canvassers can help connect you with vital resources.

- Organizing and project management: You may have a great handle on mixing browns and greens, but what about mixing schedules, people, supply shopping, and to-do lists? If just reading that sentence made your stomach turn, tap your peers to find a master organizer.

- E-mail and social media: You're a pro at posting pictures of your pup on Facebook, but creating a brand voice, managing messaging, and fielding feedback from your fans may be a bit beyond your expertise. Good thing there are plenty of people who are social-media maestros.

- Web design and development: A website goes a long way in promoting your project and educating your community, but for you, HTML is more like HTMhell. Invite coders and creatives to make your Web presence shine while you focus on managing microbes.

- Fund-raising: Would some donated dollars make a whole lotta sense (or cents) for your endeavor? Turn to entrepreneurial types who have a talent for tapping wallets, grabbing grants, and nabbing awards.

- Event planning: Sharing knowledge, experience, and best practices is one of the best parts of community compost projects. Party-hearty and socially savvy folks can help ensure that your workshop, fundraiser, or volunteer day is flawless, not a flop.

- Legal counsel: If you're not fluent in legalese, enlist a lawyer to help translate. A little legal advice can go a long way toward protecting your project—and you—from the fine print. Plus, lawyers may point out vital details you never considered before.

- Photography, videography, writing: Enlist talented shutterbugs, videographers, and wordsmiths to document your compost do-gooding so you have memories to share. Great media can fuel PR efforts, enhance your website, boost fund-raising endeavors, and keep community members (that is, potential donors or volunteers) abreast of your work.

Get the most out of volunteers by having them fill needs where their passion lies. When getting to know your compost troops, it helps to inquire about the following:

- Contact information
- Interests
- Skills
- Availability
- Limitations, such as physical issues (bad back) or concerns (fear of worms)

COMPOST'S CLASS ACT

The University of Arizona's Compost Cats provide a purrfect example of how student passion, perseverance, and organization can lead to epic social change. This collective of human (not feline) student composters sink their claws into not only all of the preconsumer food waste produced by the campus's kitchens but also the student leftovers from campus restaurant meals.

The Compost Cats were initially funded by the university's Green Fund, which stems from a small tuition addition that was proposed and approved by students to fund sustainability efforts. As the Cats expanded, they got additional support through grants and awards. Now on the road to fiscal independence, the Cats have a thriving business model processing scraps from local businesses in their large-scale operations.

Some of their finished product is sold to local residents. The rest is donated to school gardens, the university's community garden, and the Community Food Bank of Southern Arizona's backyard gardening program for low-income families.

Here's Chester F. Phillips, Compost Cats project director, on how they did it and how you can too:

"It was originally an undergraduate student idea in 2010. There was a lot of food waste coming out of our student union and compostable waste from campus landscaping and nonbiohazardous animal bedding. It was all ending up in landfills.

"The first thing I did was have a lot of meetings with the dining services staff and facilities management, finding out how all the food scraps were being handled. Where were the loading docks at the student union? How do we get buy-in not just from a student group but from staff? It has been a really broad collaboration. I spent most of the fall of 2010 talking and listening.

"The first decision we made was to start with preconsumer food scraps from the university kitchens. We would wait until that was running smoothly, then start with some postconsumer bins and signage, guiding people on how to sort—which we didn't do for another year and a half. Businesses that are not affiliated with the university began hearing about us and getting in touch, so we also serve private businesses in Tucson. Every time a new commercial business joins, we try to find out what they are paying in trash fees. If we can undercut that a little bit to sustain our program, it provides a built-in financial incentive for the business. The grant writing . . . we wouldn't exist without it.

"The Compost Cats student staff are trained to operate a tractor, a skip loader, the compost turner, and a big water tank. We are the state of Arizona's land grant institution, so we work with the campus agricultural center to use some of their equipment. We purchased our own large-scale soil screener and skip loader. We compost in a big windrow system and have a good soil-testing kit to monitor nutrient levels. We monitor temperature every day to make sure we are above the 130-degree threshold for a period of days so we are killing weed seeds and pathogens.

"We run six days a week, through the summer and winter breaks. We have a core group of paid student staff, because we didn't feel that it would work to use volunteers if we were going to hold students accountable for being places on time. They do everything from giving presentations to managing the sale and donation of the compost to doing the actual farm work and making of the compost.

"Students have a lot of leverage and power, and they have to learn how to use it. Part of my job is running a campus sustainability internship program. It's basically like a class. We start off with basic things like: here is the authority structure of the University of Arizona. We do a lesson in e-mail etiquette, because if you are going to do business with the king, you have to speak the king's tongue.

"Students in the university are kind of analogous to citizens in local government. It doesn't take many citizens getting together lobbying and agitating for something to get the attention of local government officials, especially if you are well coordinated and well spoken and communicating clearly.

"I think it's fine to have a world-changing agenda. But you have to introduce it gradually and ask, 'What can we do stepwise, who can we work with to make this possible?'

"Be relentless. There are setbacks, there are times when you don't get the funding you hoped for. But the lesson is that we can never stop asking for the change that we know we need."

For more info, go to: www.compostcats.com.

Pitching Your Compost Project to the Community

You've figured out an amazing plan to get your compost project off the ground. Now, if only you can convince Mr., Ms., and Group X to sign on.

Over the course of community composting, you're sure to bump elbows with a range of people who will definitely have an opinion on your project. If you need their help, support, funding, permission, or other input and insight, you'll have to woo them with the wonders of composting—and with assurances that your project will run as smooth as a worm's backside. Here are tips on getting it done.

- Share success stories: Nothing says "Yes, we can!" better than pointing out "See, they did!" Presenting evidence of similar groups pulling off plans similar to yours without a hitch will definitely put some concrete faces and numbers behind your pitch. Do your homework and provide lots of details.

- Read their minds: Put yourself in the shoes of the people to whom you're pitching your compost project. Aside from obvious concerns of smell, pests, and general management, what other questions might they have? Anticipate any quirky questions they might pose and have an answer ready for them, if possible: "Will the compost make me sick?" "Will this attract vagrants?" "My window is above the proposed pile space. How will this affect my quality of life?"

- Manage expectations: Be clear about what you have to offer and what you may need from the people you are pitching. What aspects of the project will you and your team be responsible for providing? What, if anything, is expected of the person(s) you're pitching and any third-party speciality, such as waste haulers or landscapers?

- Set milestones: Keeping tabs may seem a little persnickety, but it's actually a wonderful way to make sure everyone stays in communication and up-to-date on your progress. It's also a good way to get a realistic idea of how quickly and effectively your project is running. Periodic check-ins are a great way to assess progress, exchange ideas, and improve everyone's expectations all around.

- Know the law: Rules come in all sizes and scales, from the "Friday fridge clean out" mandate at work to municipal health codes and waste removal laws. Make sure you're familiar with how systems work where you intend to compost so you can answer questions and assure the community that the project adheres to legal guidelines and is on the up-and-up.

GET SCHOOLED

Sometimes all you need is a mother's love . . . of sustainability.

When five moms on the Upper West Side of Manhattan hatched a plan to get food waste composted at their children's schools, they had no idea they were launching a revolution that would eventually be adopted by New York City's Department of Sanitation and rolled out to hundreds of city schools.

As members of the District 3 Green Schools Group, Emily Fano, Pamela French, Lisa Maller, Jennifer Prescott, and Laura Sametz met monthly with other local parents to swap strategies on how to make their children's schools more sustainable. After successfully switching from Styrofoam to compostable lunch trays, these women were determined to complete the cycle and make sure those trays—and the leftover food waste on them—did get composted.

Together they hatched and executed a detailed pilot program that would eventually win two Golden Apple Awards from the city and springboard New York's first large-scale school composting program.

Here Pamela and Lisa share their experience at the Anderson School and some of the key steps, tips, and strategies that helped them succeed.

Nabbing an Organics Hauler

Lisa: "We met a consultant to a private hauler who was working with them to increase compostable collections from businesses. They offered to collect the school waste for free for a very short period of time because they wanted to prove that it would work. We saw it as an opportunity. Free collection? Let's take it and prove it can work!"

Training the Troopers: Getting Kids Involved

Lisa: "The Trash Troopers are a unique model that is now being copied by other schools in the city. We have two volunteers from each class per month. They are trained at the beginning of every month to stand up for the last ten minutes of lunch to supervise what goes into each trash can. That was one of our really big successes because you have kids teaching other kids; it comes from their peers rather than an adult. At the beginning we had an intensive adult presence to make sure everything got off on a good foot. Then it was just spot checking."

Pamela: "We made badges for them, laminated ones they wore around their necks. In terms of giving them ownership, we made it fun. They felt special that they had something that notarized who they were. I was in the lunchroom with Lisa with a bullhorn, singing songs and teaching them how to compost: 'What goes in the blue bin?' We were in the classrooms, we trained the Trash Troopers once a month."

Getting Adults Involved

Lisa: "We went into the cafeteria kitchen, to the custodial staff, and told them about our new program. The teachers have a meeting with the assistant principal, so we went to that meeting and trained them. We also trained parent volunteers."

Pamela: "We had really amazing custodians who were as excited as we were. They would help us. It was so fun, really! You need dedicated people. We threw a little ceremony and congratulated all of the adults for coming on board, like the custodial staff, the people who took the garbage out. We made them feel special."

Make This Work for You

Lisa: "Tailor it to your own school. Adapt the message, the signage, your outreach strategy to fit your audience. Constant repetition and reinforcement in the early stages of rolling out the program are key to its success. And check in periodically! Visuals are so important. We made our own signs with photographs of things that kids have for lunch, easily identifiable objects. If you have a video, post it on the school website; if people have questions, they can watch it. You can assign it as homework. There are multiple pathways to get the message out."

Gathering Metrics

Lisa: "If you can prove that your project can work on a small scale, you have a better chance of making a case and getting it adopted on a broader scale. If you don't document your project, how is it ever going to expand beyond your little community or school? We had to quantify it. We took before-and-after measurements, crunched the numbers, did graphs and pie charts. Then we had something. It was the numbers that spoke. We went from, whatever, fifty-four bags of garbage to eight. Literally, their jaws dropped, because to the city, that's money."

Secure Funding

Lisa: "Look for funding opportunities. There are lots of small grants out there for composting, recycling, and other related things. If your PTA doesn't have the money, look for opportunities and awards. There are lots of green-school awards out there. If you win an award, it can help you get the next grant or the parent support."

Fund-Raising

If you're short on green (and not the banana-peel kind), a fund-raiser might be just what your project needs. There are all sorts of ways to raise cash for the costs involved with a community-scale compost project, and they can easily be adapted to appeal to a vast range of audiences. Here are some of the things you can do to subsidize your compost-empire dreams:

- Sell your compost or other related products such as potting soil, seedlings dressed with compost, compost teas, or worms. Keep in mind that there may be regulations around the sale of these sorts of products, so check in with local sanitation, health, or commerce laws to be sure.
- Provide a service, such as picking up compostables or maintaining a garden. If you plan to pick up, check local waste-hauling regulations to make sure it's cool to cart scraps.
- Throw a fund-raising event: Everyone likes a good party, and throwing a fund-raiser not only raises cash but also brings like-minded people together to *ooh* and *ahh* over how fantastic your project is. Plus, many local businesses, artists, and performers may donate their goods and services to enhance an event or for an auction or raffle.
- Get sponsors: If you offer to publicize the support of local businesses or individuals, they may be willing to cough up some dough.

- Crowdfunding: Sites such as kickstarter.com, indiegogo.com, and rockethub.com provide tools for you to send your project into the social sphere and reach backers all around the globe.

PULLING IT ALL TOGETHER: THE ZEN OF COMMUNITY COMPOSTING

Between scheduling, staffing, and managing your compost project, you'll have a lot to learn once you're up and running. You'll likely hit a few bumps, a fair share of drama, and an occasional horror story where you expected X and got a whole lot of why, *why*, WHY?

Take a breath, and learn to take a lot more of them. It's just scraps decomposing in a pile with a little help from you and your friends, right? Baby steps will get you where you need to be, so don't try to take giant, grown-up leaps when you're just starting out. Learn from others—be open to the knowledge, resources, and assistance your community can provide you.

COMMUNITY SOUL CYCLE

Across the nation, bike-bound composters are having a wheelie good time playing with food scraps. Groups such as Vermont's One Revolution; L.A. Compost; Austin's East Side Compost Peddlers; and Raleigh, North Carolina's CompostNow provide bike-powered food-waste pickup and composting services to create black gold. (Even kids are in on this bike-centered biz. See page 183 for more.)

Gainesville Compost is one such group that has integrated with many facets of the gardening and foodie community in this Florida town. Here's the founder, Chris Cano, on what he does and how it's changed him:

"I got my undergrad at the University of Florida, and my roommates and I were really into gardening in our small backyard. We were all vegetarians, and I was amazed that we could make soil, creating a full circle of sustainability in gardening.

We had a worm bin going, but we were like, how can we do more? I had friends in restaurants bring me containers with scraps. One friend would bike it over, and that was the seed, the beginning.

"I was really disturbed by all the stuff I saw as valuable [and that] it was being thrown away. I got a bike trailer—I loved that it was a zero-emissions form of transportation—and decided to do a pilot program. I decided to start a little herb garden at a restaurant called the Midnight. We made a raised garden out of recycled wine bottles from the bar, with recycled beer and bottle caps to decorate the edges. We reclaimed wood from the dumpsters. We grew kale and lettuce and basil. One of the restaurants where we helped get a garden going has what we call our Soil Food Garden Amendment on their shelves for sale.

"We have nine spaces where organizations or community gardens have agreed to let us host a composting system on their site. We turn and manage the systems and add the new material. Then we share a portion of what we produce with them. We have agreements with our community-composting partners that define what the expectations are, that they are assigning us this place on their property and we are responsible for managing that space. We do it in exchange for promoting them as part of our mission, as well as giving them soil amendments.

"I think it's important to emphasize the idea of keeping waste in the community and doing things small-scale but using the strength of a network to make a big impact. One of the things we really want to promote is the community-building part of this and the fact that waste is not something that we need to be averse to. It can be something we bring back to the community that produced it for the benefit of that community. This is a way to create community resilience.

"I never anticipated how beneficial it would be to have this network of community members. We are able to solve so many problems that we have in our business by reaching out to all of our community partners. It's a great approach to take when you are a bootstrapper and you don't have large capital. What you have to do is build relationships and figure out how to solve problems in creative ways. That is what this network has allowed us to do."

For more information visit http://gainesvillecompost.com.

10 JOIN THE GREEN PARTY: ECO-TAINING

Do you love entertaining friends, family, and kids? Then eco-tain while you entertain.

Social gatherings are a great way to introduce composting to a captive audience. It's like putting a pretty green bow on a package that some people might otherwise never open—and making it even more palatable when offered alongside hors d'oeuvres, margaritas, and cupcakes galore.

Compost can fit into any fete in several different ways.

- Collect compostables from food, drink, and decor.
- Incorporate compost-themed activities for yourself and your guests.
- Devote a session of your book club, movie night, or family day to green-themed media or volunteering at a garden or compost project.

IT'S MY PARTY AND I'LL COMPOST IF I WANT TO

A special day is just around the corner and you've decided that you want not only to throw the best bash ever but to compost anything you can.

The first thing you will need to do is figure out exactly what you intend to compost, and where. When planning, know your limits. If you can ferment only five gallons of scraps in your sole bokashi bucket or if the urban farm up the road only accepts donations of uncooked fruit and veggie scraps for their pile, then plan accordingly. It may be helpful to draw up a special menu that fits these needs.

Ask yourself:

- Can you partner with a composting community group that is always on the lookout for donated scraps?
- Is there a local composting business that you can pay to haul your organics away?
- Who will be separating out their browns and greens for composting—you, your guests, or a catering or event specialist?

If this is a just-the-host-composts event, collect compostables as you prep the spread. If you're having your event catered, have caterers cater to you. Today's food-service industry is incredibly savvy about special requests and sustainable event planning. If your goal is to create a zero- or close-to-zero-waste event, work with them on creating a menu and service plan that caters to your dream.

If you'd like guests to pitch in by separating out specific items for composting, you'll need to offer a little guidance. Read on for fun strategies to make composting a part of the party.

Composting with Guests

The trick to being a good host or hostess is to invite people to participate in composting without preaching, bullying, or making participation feel like a chore or inconvenience. You're a host, not a nanny. You want composting to enhance your event, not bring it down.

The concept of composting is still new to many, and some folks have hang-ups about food waste or trash as is (that hand-sanitizer OCD pal is one example). Make composting as effortless and engaging as you can.

Here are some party types that pair well with guest composting:

- Potlucks: Invite your cadre of culinary friends to bring a delicious dish . . . and any scraps they amass from their prep. Provide a list of compostables in advance so they bring only appropriate materials.
- Cocktail parties: Fruits, vegetables, and spices add flair and flavor to your concoctions. Stir up fruit-filled sangria, put pineapple wedges on piña coladas, or make martinis with a twist—then compost the leftovers. Napkins and toothpicks make great browns.
- BBQs and picnics: Outdoor events beg for all sorts of fresh, light, compostable foods: juicy watermelon, cold cantaloupe balls, salads galore. If you bokashi, meat-heavy grillathons will be right up your bone- and fat-filled alley.
- Kids' events: Kids and compost go together like worms and dirt. There are so many things you can do with children that an entire section is dedicated to them, starting on page 179.

Party Day!

A little bit of organization and a lot of good signage go a long way in getting your guests to compost.

First, set the tone. Inform your guests of your intentions as early as the invitation. Use welcoming, inclusive language to get them excited about it.

Then, plot the logistics. There are two scales of collection points: small and big.

Small collection sites go in places where people tend to discard items such as toothpicks, garnishes, wood stirrers, tea bags, lemon wedges, and used napkins. The bar and dessert table are great places to put collection vessels for these items. Purchase ventilated compost-collection crocks or select a pretty bowl, a cookie jar, or an elegant vase—whatever fits your budget, party theme, and decor. Circulate often to collect the contents of these receptacles so containers don't become an eyesore.

If you're going big and collecting all the food waste from your heaping Thanksgiving buffet, take some time to design a special trash station (or stations) that makes separating items easy. Each receptacle should have clear signage that guides guests regarding where to put what. Ideally, signs should be at eye level so folks see them before they succumb to the knee-jerk reaction of dumping trash into the first container they encounter. The clearer the role of the compost-collection bin is, the easier it will be for guests to know what to do.

Have fun with it. Draw pictures, make big bold letters, go all out designing your collection stations. If you're throwing a luau, put a grass skirt on your sign. If it's a birthday party, add streamers or paper pom-poms.

Compost-Friendly Party Decor

Please deposit
- Fruit garnishes
- Toothpicks
- Napkins

Sweet and discreet, use a vase or other elegant vessel to collect small compostables.

Compostables
Paper Plates
Napkins
Food scraps

Make a compost receptacle part of the decor and have fun with signage!

FAITH IN COMPOST

Each weekend, Austin's University United Methodist Church feeds brunch to hundreds of needy guests through their Open Door Ministry. What's a congregation to do with all of the compostable waste that results?

The answer to their prayers—compost it.

By coordinating a churchwide effort to separate out compostables and recyclables from landfill-bound trash, the church diverts about 225 gallons of food waste each week, or nearly 12,000 gallons per year. They've won a Keep Austin Beautiful award for recycling waste reduction and the Cool Congregations Challenge in grounds and water conservation from the Texas Interfaith Center for Public Policy.

Gay Goforth, communications leader of University United Methodist Church's Open Door Ministry, explains how they've pulled it off:

"Throughout the church and in Open Door, we have three kinds of trash receptacles: recyclable, compostable, and everything else. We bring them out to our alley, and a hauling service comes and takes them away once a week.

"Every Saturday, we serve brunch to about 250 homeless and needy people, whom we call our guests. We serve turkey and cheese quesadillas, grits, oatmeal, cold cereal, toast, fresh fruit and vegetables, hard-boiled eggs, and condiments such as peanut butter and jelly.

"Good signage and having a monitor to help people are the two giant needs that make composting work for a large group. My husband and I made stick signs with forty-two-inch heavy dowel rods that get stuck in the trash cans. They are about three and a half feet up so people can see them. On the top we have an 8½ x 11 compost sign with a little icon that says for paper napkins, paper cups. I backed the sign with a piece of green paper so it stands out and then laminated it. They have lasted very well! We also have a recycling stick sign and a regular trash stick sign.

"The whole world doesn't think in terms of plastic, paper, cardboard, compostables. People go, 'Does this count?' 'I don't know, this is waxy.' That's where your monitor comes in to help.

"We have a regular crew of about ten guest volunteers. They set up the place, they take down the tables, they mop. Then we have a giant volunteer system from the church, the University of Texas, and local high school service organizations. It's a huge volunteer contingent, and it is constantly changing. Training can be really hard if your audience constantly changes. If I am there as a leader, I have boiled it down to four sentences to explain how to deal with the trash.

"One of our regular guest volunteers had taken on the title of Recycle Technician. He was the monitor and would correct people, 'This goes here. That goes there.' He had a personal investment in this work, and he went with us when we got our first award. He felt like it was his award.

"The guests are very supportive and aware of recycling and composting. It has been really neat."

For more information, please visit www.uumc.org/open-door-ministry.

Compostable Service Ware and Decorations

Nothing says "I love you, Ma Earth" more than whipping out reusable dishware instead of a bag full of petroleum-based plastic or Styrofoam plates. However, let's be real. Your hands are chapping at the thought of washing dishes for forty guests, and besides, you have place settings only for you, your beau, and your little dog, Max. And as for your decorations, helium balloons are so fun and pretty . . . but they deflate and end up littering the earth and harming animals that eat them or get tangled in their string.

What's an earth lover to do?

To start, green your decor.

- Flowers make wonderful and colorful accents for any fete and are easily composted in any kind of pile. Float blooms alone in bowls and vases or make wreaths, arrangements, or garlands of leaves, blooms, and twigs. If you'd prefer not to cut fresh blossoms, consider pretty potted plants you can keep or give to your guests as favors.

- Light up your life with paper-bag lanterns: Forget tacky tiki torches. Create walkways and glowing accents by placing tealights on a bed of sand in brown paper bags that you purchase or collect from your own shopping excursions. After the event is over, reuse the bags or recycle or compost them.
- Choose paper over plastic: Banners, streamers, and more come in beautiful paper alternatives. Plus, it's easy to make your own paper heart, flower, and snowflake chains. DIY or store-bought paper pom-poms make a wonderful alternative to balloons and are divinely reusable. If making them, use tissue paper made from recycled paper to go eco all the way.

Compostable service ware rocks the party twice over. Not only does it come from greener pastures, but when placed in proper composting conditions, it breaks down into soil-enriching compost. Most of the petroleum-based plastic and Styrofoam counterparts can't be recycled and head to the landfill—the ultimate party pooper.

Compostable service ware is made from a range of materials:

- Paper and cardboard
- PLA, or polylactide, a corn-based plastic
- PHA, or polyhydroxy fatty acid, a corn-based plastic
- Molded pulp product, made from waste-paper materials
- Bagasse, a by-product of sugarcane- and sorghum-juice extraction
- Wheat straw
- Bamboo
- Palm fiber
- Soy, corn, tapioca, and potato starch

Nearly all compostable service ware is designed to break down at industrial-scale composting facilities only, which means that they aren't meant to decompose in your backyard pile or worm bin. At commercial sites, the scale of materials composted, the heat they generate, and the varied machines that chop, shred, and mix compostables create the opti-

mum conditions for these complex materials to break down. With the exception of nonwaxy paper, cardboard plates and napkins, or anything that is specifically labeled for backyard composting, you won't be able to compost service ware at home.

However, that doesn't mean it's futile to use them. Even if your town doesn't offer a way for you to send compostable items to an industrial-scale composting facility, "using these items is still valuable because they're made from renewable materials," says Steve Mojo, executive director of the Biodegradable Products Institute, which is the organization that awards the compostable logo to qualifying products. "As such they provide some greenhouse gas reduction."

Optimize your green purchasing power and keep an eye out for the following certifications on the products you buy:

- Biodegradable Products Institute compostable logo: These items can be composted only in large-scale composting facilities.
- USDA Certified Biobased Product label (part of the USDA BioPreferred program): This label helps you understand what your products are made of and purchase items sourced from renewable resources.
- OK Compost HOME label: This European certification identifies products that are suitable for backyard compost piles. (Not currently available in the United States.)

COMING TO AN EVENT OR CORNER NEAR YOU . . .

The NYC Compost Project hosted by Build It Green!NYC knows that if you can't bring New Yorkers to a food scrap drop-off site, you have to bring the site to them. This innovative community-compost program is all about encouraging busy city folks to compost in unexpected places, such as on their morning commute or while pedaling the annual Five Boro Bike Tour. By setting up food-scrap drop-off stations by train stops and at special events, Build It Green collects tons of what would otherwise be trash to process into black gold.

What started as a grassroots composting effort by New York City Master Composters Stephanos Koullias and Leanne Spaulding in a Queens community garden has since bloomed into a Department of Sanitation–sponsored education and compost facility.

Here's Gina Baldwin, public engagement coordinator (2013–14) for the NYC Compost Project hosted by Build It Green!NYC, on how they do it.

"We started commuter composting as a way to reach people in a different space. Traditionally, for the past few years, people in New York have been composting at greenmarkets. We're looking for nontraditional models to capture interactions with people who may not go to the greenmarket or who live in neighborhoods that don't have one. That shouldn't be a deterrent to having compost opportunities.

"It was an interesting model, and it has grown. We've expanded into more sites in Queens and Brooklyn, and the Lower East Side Ecology Center started commuter sites in Manhattan. [For more on the LESEC, see page 156.]

"Sometimes people aren't sure what it is, or ask, 'Are you here every week?' They aren't sure it is going to be a regular thing. We make it a point to communicate clearly with our audience that we are always here because there is nothing like being stranded with a bag of food scraps when you are trying to do something good. All of our drop-off sites have sign-up sheets for people to get on our monthly e-newsletter list. We also have Twitter and Facebook accounts and post in advance whenever we are going to be closing our site, which is generally on federal holidays. Even during the snowiest days during the past winter, during the polar vortex, we were still here. It helps that we are paid staff. With volunteer-run programs [there is always the risk] that people will not show up.

"Because we have [run compost programs] at several different kinds of events, we kind of know what to expect. The biggest part of doing events is knowing what kind of waste is going to be there. At a bike tour, for example, we know there will be a lot of fresh fruit peels. At an event with cooked food, people are probably going to eat most of the food, and you are going to have a lot of packaging to deal with. Sometimes we have to get different bins that are the right height and look nice. You can't use the same bins you use outdoors at a street fair for an indoor dinner party. Those are definitely things we think about.

"Some event tips? Connect with the event planners enough in advance that you can get the vendors to buy compostable materials. Plan for what you think you'll need, then have backup. We will bring a bunch of bags just in case all of our bins fill up. It's not ideal, but we don't want to be left not composting materials we committed to compost. Let the attendees know in advance so they are expecting it: 'There is going to be composting at this event! Look out for the green bins!'

"A lot of people are more comfortable [saving and dropping off their compostables] with biodegradable bags. There are alternatives to that that are less consumer intensive, like if you have paper bags at your house, or a container. But biodegradable bags make composting easier for some people. If that's what makes them participate, then we meet people where they are. In a city that is so diverse, with so much going on, where every person is different and everyone's fridge is a different size, it's really about making it work for everyone."

For more information, please visit www.bignyc.org/compost.

CHILDREN AND COMPOST ACTIVITIES

If you've got a bunch of microhuman organisms in your life, the chances are you've got some ready, willing, and deliriously enthusiastic composters on hand.

Kids of all ages make amazing composters because they're curious and quick learners. Plus, they love to play with creepy crawlies. They seem to have boundless energy that most grown-ups can only muster with an espresso (or four). When they're together in a group, kids also go a long way in overcoming their fears. Nothing like good old positive peer pressure to push each other to be brave and curious. Like the germs that circulate in their classrooms, the enthusiasm is contagious.

Plan an eco-friendly playdate or party for your children using some of the ideas below. They'll trump any afternoon with a clown, hands down.

DIY: BUILD AND DECORATE A TINY WORM HOUSE

If your worm bin is overflowing with wigglers or you've been itching for an excuse to buy another pound or two, throw a Make a Worm Bin party for your children and their friends.

The event is like arts and crafts on eco-steroids. Instead of messy macaroni art or lame lanyard bracelets, kids will leave your home with new pets in a home they built and decorated themselves.

This activity is best for parents with at least a little experience with vermicomposting, as you'll probably get a lot of questions from kids and their parents. If you don't like wrangling a large crowd of kids, you may want to skip ahead to another activity.

YOU WILL NEED:

- 1 cup of finished vermicompost for every 5 children, in its own bowl.
- Small, plastic, lidded and ventilated container for each of your guests, which will serve as their worm house. A quart size is a nice starter, but any container will do. Purchase cute storage containers, upcycle take-out or Tupperware containers, or encourage guests to bring their own. It doesn't matter, as long as they are high-enough quality plastic for you to drill 5–10 ventilation holes through the lid. Transparent plastics are fine and make for great observation.
- Browns and bedding. Prepare enough newspaper strips to fill each child's container.
- Several spritzing bottles, filled with water. Don't use bottles that previously held chemicals or cleaners. If you don't want to spritz bedding with the children, then premoisten it ahead of time.
- About 50 worms per child, based on a 1-quart (think, large soup) take-out container. Presort the worms in separate containers, or let the children pick

their own worms out of several piles you provide them. The latter can be a lot of fun.

- Recognizable feedstock, such as chopped-up banana peels or strawberry tops, previously frozen and thawed.
- Stickers to decorate the bin.
- Name tags for the containers or individualized bags so they can take their mini-worm bin home.
- Care instruction sheets with the basic tips on keeping the worms happy and healthy. Need a guideline? Take notes from chapter 6.

PARTY TIME!

It's the big day. Organize your guests at tables or in a circle on the floor and begin:

1. Pass around your compost samples and have the kids feel, smell, and examine them. Introduce the concept of composting by asking questions: What do you think this is? What is it used for? Where does soil come from? Where do your fruit and vegetable scraps go after you eat them? Who can name something that will turn into compost? The main takeaways to drive home are that this "dirt" (nearly everyone's first guess) is special stuff called compost and is a supernutritious food for soil. It comes from fruits, vegetables, and plant matter that have broken down into important nutrients. Soil needs to be healthy so plants can grow big and strong.

2. Introducing . . . red wigglers! Put a few worms in your hand and let the kids touch and examine them. Encourage them not to be shy but understand that some kids may be too timid to jump in just yet. Ask them what they know about worms. Explain how worms are a huge part of making the amazing compost superfood the kids just encountered. Take some fun facts from chapter 6 to share with the kids. If you come across any baby worms, be sure to share them. Kids go nuts over the tiny, pink pals.

3. Distribute the worm houses, bedding, and worms. Invite the kids to fill their worm houses with newspaper. Check each container, as kids all have different ideas of what constitutes full. Chat about why you need to have bedding as both food and housing for the worms. If children brought their own containers, drill airholes for them.

4. Make it rain: (If you have premoistened your bedding, you can skip to the next step.) Once the containers are filled to the top, spritz the bedding until it feels like a wrung-out sponge; if the kids are old enough, have them do it. Adjust as needed by adding spritzes or subbing in dry paper for overly drenched bins. Talk about the role water plays for your worms.

5. Bring on the wigglers: Distribute the worms and have each child drop in his or her portion. Share more wiggler basics and see how much they remember from your earlier chat.

6. Feed the worms: Provide each child a small portion of feedstock to get the worms started. For a one-quart container, you can say grape-sized cut-up portions. Explain how much to feed and how often. Emphasize that they should never feed when there is still a lot of the last serving left. Remind them that as the worm population grows, they will eat lots, lots more.

7. Decorate: Once the initial thrill of meeting and adding their very own worm pets to their containers has passed (and this thrill lasts for quite some time), it's time to pretty up their habitat. Distribute plenty of stickers for the kids to go wild with.

8. Label each bin with the child's name and pack them up with a set of care instructions.

You did it! Now watch the worm empire spread. If you'd like to keep in touch with your network of new wormers, start an e-mail chain with the children's parents to exchange tips and updates. Or share a digital photo album on a site such as Facebook. Since you're the pro wormer of the bunch, make sure to supply your contact information to anyone who might have questions for you.

TYKES AND BIKES

In Traverse City, Michigan, one boy has mixed his love of composting and biking with an entrepreneurial streak. Carter Schmidt, with the help of his dad, Ty, built a business biking around town and picking up buckets of compostable waste from clients. He launched Carter's Compost when he was just seven years old and has hauled an average of four hundred pounds of scraps a week since. In 2013 the company won Grand Traverse County's Take It Back "Recycler of the Year" award.

Carter's Compost is all about spreading the compost love, which includes a range of educational opportunities, shared neighborhood compost piles, and helping other kids launch and build their bike-based compost businesses.

Here are Ty and Carter Schmidt on how they do it:

Carter: "I think composting is a great job for kids because when they have a real job, they already know how to manage money and actually work. The kids in my school are like, 'You have a business? Awesome! That's so cool!' And they want to join and have all sorts of franchises and stuff.

"My favorite parts of the job are wrangling worms, screening the compost, and also riding my bike and meeting [new people]. If you don't keep your pile balanced and happy it smells gross, which is why some people don't like to compost. But if you balance your pile it won't smell at all.

"I think people like what I am doing. I will probably keep composting until I get a real job or until I go to college . . . because I can't really do it while I am in college."

Ty: "Traverse City has a population of maybe fifteen thousand people, and it's a very progressive, forward-thinking town. It's got this big foodie movement and is very grow-your-own, love-your-farmer. No one was really being the compost ambassador, and it seemed like an opportunity to spread the word.

"We have always been composters, always had bikes, and we came across a story about Bootstrap Compost in Boston. I read Carter the website, and he was all over it! He is one of those kids who are always trying to earn money and always has ideas about selling things.

"We started with Carter's old [bicycle] baby trailer. Eventually, we invested in a heavy-duty cargo trailer, and Carter spent his own money to get it. It was like eight hundred bucks! But Carter is making real money and saving for college. If he could pay his way through university, that would be pretty awesome.

"The biggest hurdle for us now is finding the space for scraps. We have started partnering with like-minded gardener friends and neighbors who have space to spare in their pile, and eco-friendly businesses that are developing these neighborhood compost stations as well. We call them sharing piles and have about fifteen of them.

"All of our [clients] get one bucket of compost, the share piles get to keep all of their compost. We also have neighborhood parties where we invite people over to screen it. We do a Tour de Pile, where we visit the compost piles, and Carter's College of Compostology, where we invite people over. We also have a bike share. We try to make education a big part of it because we can't just keep taking more members. We are trying to graduate as many people as we can into composting their own scraps.

"We have hosted a few zero-waste events at the school cafeterias and have been involved with the school gardens. Whenever we do these events in the community, we bring the worms on the bike trailer, and the kids just love it. That is their favorite part. I think it's a good tool to teach them young and start them right.

"We are youth driven and youth-centric. We have grown and helped other kids in other neighborhoods take over some of our buckets where they are. It becomes Max's Compost, or Jack's Compost. They manage their own members, their own customers. When someone e-mails us from another neighborhood, I'll forward that e-mail to Max [or Jack or whoever], and he can take them on if he wants to.

"My vision is we can get an army of kids and bikes and buckets biking around Traverse City, and that becomes the new normal. You don't see paperboys anymore, but I'd hope you could see compost boys and girls out there biking around."

For more information, visit: http://carterscompost.com.

DIY: PLANT SEEDS IN SOIL AND COMPOST

Kids love, love, love growing plants from seeds. Teach them about the benefits of compost by planting seeds in soil mixed with luscious black gold. This is a great activity if you have children and want to throw them the coolest classroom event, birthday party, or playdate on the block.

YOU WILL NEED:

- 1 small pot for every child. If your seeds will outgrow their initial homes and require repotting, consider using a compostable seed-starting pot that can be buried directly in soil.
- Garden soil
- Finished compost
- Seeds; easy sprouters include pumpkins, radishes, beans, sunflowers, and basil
- Bowl and a spoon for each child to mix compost and soil in
- Watering can
- Stickers to decorate the pots with if using nonbiodegradable pots (optional)
- Care sheet on how to care for the seeds

PARTY TIME!

Your guests are ready and giving this activity a big green thumbs-up. Let's get planting!

1. Provide each child with a pot, a bowl, and a spoon.
2. Distribute a pot's worth of soil to each child's bowl. Ask the children what they know about soil and the role it plays in helping plants grow. Ask them to observe, touch, and smell the soil and share details of everything they see.
3. Bring on the compost: Circulate a bowl of fresh finished compost and ask them if they know what it is, what is does, and how it's made. Fill in the

blanks if they can't guess the answers. Their main takeaway should be that this isn't just soil—it's a supercharged soil vitamin that will help plants grow big and strong.

4. Drop a couple of spoonfuls of compost into each child's bowl. Ask the children to stir it up good, because this is the food that will help their little seeds grow.

5. Transfer the finished potting mix to their pots.

6. Distribute the seeds: Let the children decide what they want to grow from a variety of choices, or decide in advance and give everyone the same seeds. For small, leafy greens, give them 5 to 10 seeds. For big plants such as beans or sunflowers, provide 2 or 3. Having more than one seed will increase the chances of successful germination.

7. Show the children how to make ½-inch deep holes in the soil using the tips of their spoon handles. Make sure the holes aren't too deep because seeds germinate best when closer to the surface. Ask them to make as many holes as they have seeds, spread out across their pot. They should insert a seed in each hole and cover it up.

8. Decorate nonbiodegradable pots with stickers.

9. Send the children home with their new pots and care instructions on watering, sunlight needs, and replanting big, burly seedlings.

Compost Explorers

There's no need to journey to the center of the earth when the center of your compost system is just as fascinating. Give a tour of your compost system and invite the kids to help out Ma Earth. It's no secret that kids make great free labor, because what feels like a chore to adults is usually a grand old time for kids. Have them add greens and browns, sift compost, monitor temperatures, and add compost to your garden or plants. Got a worm bin? See if you can find worms, count cocoons, and harvest black gold. Nothing seems wackier or more fun to a child than learning about caring for a pile of garbage and its wiggly, wild inhabitants.

How do you wrangle a roster of young composters? If you don't have kids of your own, consider offering to babysit your friends' kids or inviting a social club and the members' kids over for an educational and fun afternoon. As long as you let people know what you'll be doing and how fun it will be, the event can be pitched in an appealing way. Throwing in a pizza or other tasty bites can help seal the deal.

Kid-Friendly Snacks That Celebrate Soil

While a fab fruit salad or crudité platter is a nice nod to the gifts borne of compost, drive your celebration of this magical process home with edible homages to compost.

SNACK ATTACK: DIY WORMS IN DIRT

Worms in Dirt is a flexible recipe that mixes gummy worms into an assortment of foods for colorful, tasty fun. The DIY version ups the ante on create-your-own-sundae parties. The concept is simple and can be tailored to your specific palate. This snacktivity is even more fun after a compost-related lesson because kids will be able to connect their dessert ingredients with the soil ecosystem they just learned about.

YOU WILL NEED:

- Bowls or parfait cups. Clear ones allow children to admire the layers in their "dirt."
- Spoons
- Gummy worms
- A range of dirt-themed ingredients, including but not limited to the following suggestions:
    - Crumbled brownie or chocolate cake "soil"
    - Nut "pebbles"

- Sprinkles "bacteria"
- Coconut flake "fungi"
- Chopped fruit salad "compost greens"
- Granola "browns"
- Pudding or frosting "mud"
- Kiwi slice or mint "leaves"
- Graham cracker "cardboard browns"
- Edible flowers

PARTY TIME!

When it's time for dessert, set up the ingredients in a buffet-style line. Tell the kids it's time to make Worms in Dirt and explain all the amazing ingredients that await them. Then line them up and invite them to make their way down the spread, adding all of their favorite ingredients to their bowls.

LET THEM EAT *MORE* WORMS: RED (GRAPE) WRIGGLERS

Want a healthy worm-shaped snack? Make adorable red (grape) wigglers. They're cute, easy to make, and a delicious, nutritious mouthful for guests of any age.

YOU WILL NEED:

- 1 or 2 bunches red seedless grapes
- Small kebab skewers
- Vanilla frosting
- Mini chocolate chips

MAKING THE GRAPE WIGGLERS

1. Wash your grapes and remove the stems.
2. Fill your skewer with grape "worm segments."

3. Make sure the last grape, which serves as the worm head, is not punctured all the way through.

4. Put two vanilla-frosting dots on the head and place a chocolate chip in each to create worm eyes. (Yeah, yeah, worms don't really have eyes, but hey, it's a party and anything goes.)

5. Freeze (optional).

Want to upgrade this snack for adults? Soak the grapes overnight in your favorite wine or vodka. Toss them in a little sugar before you freeze them.

A delicious snack enjoyed chilled, frozen, or presoaked in booze.

Let Them Eat Worms . . . Literally!

Did you know that earthworms are an incredible source of protein that is gluten-, fat-, and sugar-free? In fact, the Maori of New Zealand have long considered *noke,* comprising certain earthworm species, to be a delicacy, alongside African and Native American cultures.

Before you get all grossed out, think about it: oysters, steamers, and snails are at least as slimy and weird to consume, if not more so. And let's not even get started on the colorful, crazy, plastic, chemical insanity of most candies and kids' cereals. In this context, worms are positively mainstream.

Worms can be fried, baked, boiled, and perhaps even brûléed into recipes ranging from tacos to stews. They, like the popular bug-snack crickets, can be made into a flour that you can sprinkle into baked goods. Chocolate chip worm cookies, anyone?

Other Eco-Activities

If you're not the type to get a thrill from planning, hosting, or executing an elaborate event, no sweat. There are lots of easy ways to have good green fun with your friends while examining the place of compost in your world.

Movie Night

If a picture is worth a thousand words, imagine the conversation an entire movie can spark. There's nothing better than curling up with a giant tub of buttery popcorn, a great film, and good friends. From blockbusters to art house documentaries, there's a great crop of movies that educate, inspire, and probe audiences with environmental themes. Grab a group for a private movie screening at a home or community space. Then spend time afterward discussing the issues raised in the film and how they impact everyday urban life. Do you see solutions to the problems posed by the movie? Is there a plan of action you, as a group, can take?

If you enjoy movie night, consider throwing an ongoing film series. If your group is the snacking type, have a small bin to collect compostables at each event.

Here are a few great flicks to get you started:

- *Dirt! The Movie* (2009). Dig into how the world has gone from caring for to destroying the soil in this probing documentary.
- *The Garden* (2008). Witness the plight of a thriving fourteen-acre community garden in L.A. that is threatened by a powerful developer determined to destroy it.
- *An Inconvenient Truth* (2006). Al Gore's Oscar-winning documentary about the effect of global warming on the planet is still topical today.
- *No Impact Man: The Documentary* (2009). A Manhattan man changes his family's lifestyle for an entire year in an attempt to live with no impact on the environment.

- *Symphony of the Soil* (2012). This artful documentary examines different soil climates and explores how composting can combat the depleting effects of industrial agriculture.
- *Wall-E* (2008). In the distant future, a robot named Wall-E cleans up an abandoned, trash-filled Earth. With friends, he sparks a revolution to change the destiny of Earth and humankind. (Great for kids.)

Day Trips, Volunteer Opportunities, and Green City Fun

The great thing about living in a city is the access you have to all the passionate, smart, creative, and dedicated people who live there. Special-interest groups and institutions regularly invite the public to share in their work, learn about their field, or simply enjoy their offerings. Oftentimes these events are free to the public and are a great way to connect with like-minded individuals.

While the following suggestions don't focus exclusively on composting, they touch the larger social ecosystem that supports and benefits from the movement.

- Volunteer: Many green city groups such as community gardens often have volunteer days when the public is invited to lend a hand. Search the Web or contact gardens nearby and spend a Saturday harvesting vegetables, building raised garden beds, or turning a compost system.
- Visit a farmers market: Oh, the sights, smells, and flavors! Your local farmers market is a great place to get in touch with what's growing right now, right near you. Chat with farmers about their soil and growing practices. Ask bakers, butchers, and cheese mongers about their artisanal styles of preparing food. Then shop, shop, shop and cook up an amazing meal. The more you know about the food you eat and the people who bring it to you, the more you'll enjoy it.
- Attend an educational event: Museums, green groups, libraries, parks departments, and more host lectures, films, panels, and demonstrations that

probe the cutting edge in their fields. Mingle with the top minds in the movement.

- Have a picnic in a park: Sure, there are skate parks, sculpture parks, and too many car parks. But remember the good old-fashioned kind, with trees, grass, rocks, and perhaps even a fountain or stream? Pack up some snacks, games, and/or a good book and head to the great outdoors for some R & R among the urban wild.

- Join a CSA: Community-supported agriculture shares are a great way to contribute to the growth of a local organic farm and get fresh-picked, seasonal produce. In addition to meeting new people at your produce pickups and during volunteer hours, CSAs offer opportunities to visit the farm. Help with a harvest and see your food growing in a field.

RESOURCES

To learn more about composting, soil, and good green living, check out some of my favorite resources:

Books + Magazines

Mary Appelhof, *Worms Eat My Garbage: How to Set Up and Maintain a Worm Composting System* (Flowerfield Enterprises, 1997).

BioCycle. Both a print and online magazine and host to several conferences a year, *BioCycle* is the official publication of the US Composting Council. www.biocycle.net

Stu Campbell, *Let It Rot: The Gardener's Guide to Composting* (Storey Books, 1998).

Adam Footer, *Bokashi Composting: Scraps to Soil in Weeks* (New Society Publishers, 2014).

Jeff Lowenfels and Wayne Lewis, *Teaming with Microbes: The Organic Gardener's Guide to the Soil Food Web* (Timber Press, 2010).

Barbara Pleasant and Deborah L. Martin, *The Complete Compost Gardening*

Guide: Banner Batches, Grow Heaps, Comforter Compost, and Other Amazing Techniques for Saving Time and Money, and Producing the Most Flavorful, Nutritious Vegetables Ever (Storey Publishing, 2008).

Ben Raskin, *Compost: A Family Guide to Making Soil from Scraps, with Games, Stickers, and More!* (Roost Books, 2014). Great for kids!

Urban Farm Magazine. A fun publication for hobbyists and enthusiasts learning the ropes of urban agriculture. www.urbanfarmonline.com

Blogs, Websites, Online Magazines

The NYC Compost Project. This is just one of many amazing online resources for small-scale composting and Master Composter certification. (It's my alma mater, so it gets a special shout-out.) Look for similar types of programs near you. www.nyc.gov/compostproject

Red Worm Composting. This blog by Bentley Christie is personable and packed with info, DIY building plans, and lots of vermiculture experiments. www.redwormcomposting.com

Treehugger. An expansive online news portal that covers everything green from technology to transportation. http://www.treehugger.com

The United States Composting Council. This nonprofit trade and professional organization has a wealth of information on large-scale operations, compost news and technology, and many local resources. http://compostingcouncil.org

United States Environmental Protection Agency. The EPA sets the standard for best practices when it comes to Ma Earth. Read about composting, pet waste, sustainability, and more. www.epa.gov

Vermicomposters.com. Wanna swap pics and stories of your little wigglers and their poop piles? Check out this social network for worming enthusiasts with forums, blogs, and photos. http://vermicomposters.com

Advocacy + Research Organizations

EM Research Organization. EMRO, based in Japan, is the center of effective microorganism technology. www.emrojapan.com

The Food Tank. Focused on sustainable ways to alleviate hunger and food insecurity, The Food Tank provides a compelling lens through which to explore food waste. http://foodtank.com

Institute for Local Self Reliance. In addition to providing guidance on environmentally sound community building strategies, ILSR also has a Compost Initiative. www.ilsr.org

Natural Resources Defense Council. Find out about current environmental issues and advocacy movements that defend the earth. www.nrdc.org/issues

Rodale Institute. Everything you need to know about organic farming and best soil practices can be found at this research and outreach nonprofit. http://rodaleinstitute.org

Other Great Organizations Featured in Compost City

Biodegradable Products Institute (New York, NY): www.bpiworld.org

Build It Green!NYC (New York, NY): www.bignyc.org/compost

Carter's Compost (Traverse City, Mich.): http://carterscompost.com

Compost Coalition (Austin, Tex.): http://compostcoalition.com

Earth Matter (New York, NY): https://earthmatter.org

Gainesville Compost (Gainesville, Fla.): http://gainesvillecompost.com

GrowMemphis (Memphis, Tenn.): http://growmemphis.org

Growing Power (Milwaukee and Chicago): www.growingpower.org

Lower East Side Ecology Center (New York, NY): http://lesecologycenter.org

Seattle Tilth (Seattle, Wash.): http://seattletilth.org

Shig Matsukawa (New York, NY): http://recyclefoodwaste.org

University of Arizona Compost Cats (Tucson): www.compostcats.com

Woodland Park Zoo (Seattle, Wash.): www.zoo.org/conservation/zoodoo

ACKNOWLEDGMENTS

A vast ecosystem helped make this book possible. I am so very thankful to:

. . . my parents, Remedios Sioco and Foo Guey Louie, for their un-yielding support and countless bags of frozen food scraps.

. . . my agent Marilyn Allen and her gut instinct to mine black gold.

. . . my editor Rochelle Bourgault for her vision and Zen-goddess patience, copy editor DeAnna Satre for her deft eye, and Julia Gaviria for guarding the manuscript.

. . . designers Daniel Urban-Brown and Jim Zaccaria for helping to make worm poop and rotting things look sexy.

. . . Roost Books for believing in said sexiness of poop and rot.

. . . the NYC Compost Project, the Queens Botanical Garden, and my Master Composter certification instructors Dan Tainow and Julia Corwin.

. . . Leanne Spaulding for the extra set of eyes.

. . . Dave Shor, for the aha moment, and Paula Witt for the instant messages.

. . . the talents at Paragraph: Workspace for Writers for the camara-derie, co-misery, advice, and tea bags.

. . . the pioneers, educators, and experts who generously took time to share their expertise (I wish I could have included every single word of our mind-blowing talks in this book!): Gina Baldwin (also for the extra set of eyes), Charlie Bayrer, Chris Cano, Christine Datz-Romero, Marisa DeDominicis, Judy Elliott, Pamela French, Jeff Gage, Gay Goforth, Susan Greenfield, Sheri Hinshaw, Heather-Nicole Hoffman, Lisa Maller, Shig Matsukawa, Steven Mojo, Chris Peterson, Chester F. Phillips, Ty Schmidt, Carter Schmidt, Carl Woestwin.

. . . and last, Chris Clement, who made beautiful digital versions of my analogue drawings and never flinched at the compost experiments in the cupboards. You are my worm wrangler and best friend. I could not have done any of this without you.

Worm on!

INDEX

Roost Books
An imprint of Shambhala Publications, Inc.
Horticultural Hall
300 Massachusetts Avenue
Boston, Massachusetts 02115
roostbooks.com

9 8 7 6 5 4 3 2 1

First Edition
Printed in the United States of America

⊗This edition is printed on acid-free paper that meets
the American National Standards Institute Z39.48 Standard.
♻This book is printed on 30% postconsumer recycled paper.
For more information please visit www.shambhala.com.

Distributed in the United States by Penguin Random House LLC
and in Canada by Random House of Canada Ltd

Title page cityscape created by Jim Zaccaria
Interior designed by James D. Skatges
Illustrations by Rebecca Louie and Chris Clement

Library of Congress Cataloging-in-Publication Data

Louie, Rebecca.
Compost city: practical composting know-how for small-space living/
Rebecca Louie.—First edition.
    pages   cm
Includes bibliographical references and index.
ISBN 978-1-61180-220-7 (alk. paper)
1. Compost. I. Title. II. Title: Practical composting know-how
for small-space living.
S661.L68 2015
631.8'75—dc23
2014028101

ABOUT THE AUTHOR

Rebecca Louie, a certified Master Composter, is also a journalist, bee-keeper, and friend to all worms. She divides her time between New York City and the Catskill Mountains. To learn more about Rebecca and her work, please visit rebeccalouie.com and thecompostess.com.